T0146825

Poor Lofdoc's Almanac

Short and Sweet

Lofdoc (Lots of Fishing Doc)

authorHOUSE®

AuthorHouse™
1663 Liberty Drive
Bloomington, IN 47403
www.authorhouse.com
Phone: 1 (800) 839-8640

Published by AuthorHouse 07/20/2016

ISBN: 978-1-5246-1603-8 (sc)
ISBN: 978-1-5246-1604-5 (hc)
ISBN: 978-1-5246-1602-1 (e)

Library of Congress Control Number: 2016910368

Print information available on the last page.

Contents

PROLOG IX

A HELPING HAND 1

A LETTER 4

A PICTURE 6

A TERRIFYING EVENING.. 8

BE PATIENT, BE PATIENT! 11

BIRDS, BIRDS, BIRDS 13

BRAIN, BRAWN OR, SKILL 15

CHARITY 18

CONGRATULATIONS.. 20

CRYING OUT IN THE WILDERNESS 22

EDUCATION.. 25

EXCUSES... 28

FIDELITY... 31

GIVING THANKS 33

GOING HOME... 35

GREETINGS AND SALUTATIONS 38

HANGIN IN THERE 41

HOME FOR CHRISTMAS 44

HOME IS WHERE THE HEART IS........................... 47

HORNETS 49

HUMILITY 53

INTEGRITY.. 56

KINDNESS... 59

LIFE'S TIMELINES...61

LONELINESS 64

MEMORIAL DAY.. 67

MEMORIES LOST 70

MEMORIES OF YEASTERYEARS............................. 72

MOURNING DOVES 77

MY BROTHER'S KEEPER 79

OLT TOO SOON SCHMART TOO LATE 82

"OUT OF THE BLUE" 85

PERSEVERANCE 89

QUACKERY 93

REINCARNATION OF A SINGER 97

RELUCTANTLY, HE HANDED OVER THE KEY 102

SO YOU WANT TO BE AN AUTHOR 105

SOUPS ON! 108

THANK - YOU 110

THE CLOCK -- A CONTINUUM 113

THE DAY AFTER CHRISTMAS (DAY) 117

THE EASTER BASKET HUNT 119

THE FOUR PICTURE STORY 122

THE GREEN-EYED MONSTER 129

THE IMPORTANCE OF BEING IMPORTANT 132

THE LIFE AND LOVES OF JAZZY 135

THE LOVE STORY 137

THE PASSAGE OF TIME 140

THE REDEYED DRUMMER 143

THE RELUCTANT HEALER 146

THE RHODODENDRON AFFAIR 149

THE ROSE OF SHARON 153

THE SAND DOLLAR 155

THE SINGER 159

THE SWAN 162

THE TEN ARMED SWIMMER 164

THE WORLD OF YESTERYEAR 167

THINGS HAPPEN 170

THINKING MAKES IT SO 172

TREASURES OF A NURSING HOME 174

WE ALL HAVE DREAMS 177

WELCOME 180

WHAT GOES AROUND, COMES AROUND 182

WHEN DID IT ALL START? 185

WHEN THE SUN GOES DOWN 189

WHY, AND WHEN, TO WRITE A BOOK..................................193
SO, WHY CAN'T WE DREAM? 196
WINNERS AND LOSERS OF THE WORLD.............................198
YOU ARE MY SUNSHINE 200
YOU NEVER KNOW 203

Prolog

A humble and grateful confession!

Many months ago, when I had completed, and had published my third book LOFDOC'S STORIES SHORT AND SWEET with the subtitle An Octogenarian's oracles, I was asked the question "Will this, your third book, be your final contribution to the world of literature?" I responded by saying "I would love to continue exploring new vistas, but the laws of nature will always have the final say; after all, I am, 89 years old."

Well, now, `the rest of the story`.

I guess I am no different than anyone else; after all, we are all birds of a feather, are we not? When the mountain climber was asked "Why do you climb mountains; his answer --"because it is there"; and so it is with me -- I write, because, I am still here. But, I confess, I reverently hoped that I would `still be around` to continue to tell you --- `the rest` of my stories.

So yes, dear reader, I have poured many hours of pure joy into this, my fourth book. There are stories titled: ` Crying out in the wilderness`; The ten Armed Swimmer; Quackery; The Sand dollar; Treasures of a nursing home, etc. I have tried to be accurate, sincere, and entertaining, I have given you a new world of thoughts and remembrances that you will hopefully embrace and enjoy. I sincerely believe this, my fourth volume, represents the best of all my lifetime literary efforts.

I hope you will embrace and enjoy my little stories, as much as I have loved writing them. I now, give you, Lofdoc's fourth book ---

POOR LOFDOC'S 'ALMANAC' --- SHORT AND SWEET

Lofdoc

Oh, by the way, perhaps you might want to know about my use of the name, LOFDOC, as my pseudonym? No secret, I love fishing, so--- LOTS --OF -- FISHING -- DOC; Yes, I am a retired Doctor of medicine. I had practiced medicine (solo), for over thirty years, in Ohio. I now devote most of my time caring for my medically wounded Angel, wife, of 65 years.

Andrew Opritza, MD FACP

A HELPING HAND

Recently, I had written a whimsical short story about a swimmer with ten arms titled, `the ten armed swimmer`. It is a lowly (simple) story about the life and adventures of a squid – yes, a squid – it is just an interesting story, with a fetching title. But, the story I am about to relate to you, has much more substance and human emotions intertwined—with -- `a helping hand` and kindness.

One need not look too far afield, to read or hear of a story documenting someone's kindness – heralding `a helping hand` performing a good deed. Needless to say, `the everyday` `helping hand`, such as helping someone carry a package, or opening a door for someone, is appreciated and welcome; but, every so often, a helping hand, is so much more; it is an act of love performed without hesitation, or concern, for personal welfare and safety; -- more -- anon.

The "Helping hand," may not even be a hand; the helping hand may be a smile that helps penetrate the deep gloom of a person in despair. "The helping hand" may be a handshake of friendship, or it may simply impart a nudge, or encouragement to a faltering friend's need for understanding and support. And, not the least important, a helping financial hand may be, at times, a critical life saver.

One need only visit a hospital, a nursing home, or a home for the indigent, to affirm that the aphorism `but for the grace of God, go I`, is alive and well today; the human spirit of caring, understanding, and brotherly love can be seen, at every turn of life's journey.

But, hold on, as in most life riddles, there are twists and turns that often muddle, even more, life's realities. Yes, there may be many gentle, extended helping hands, but sadly, the very persons (the elderly and infirmed), that are most in need of support and caring are the very ones, who, willingly, reject the kindness extended to them. It appears that the elderly population may be said to be either, of an "independent" or "dependent" frame of mind; the latter group do blessedly, and gladly, accept the offered helping hand. Tragically, the `independent` senior citizen *will not* "Cry out in the wilderness" (crying out to the world around him for help); no, it isn't because he / she rejects kindness, and the mercy of the helping hand, but right or wrong, believes, that he / she should not be a burden to the ones they love. However, if one would look closely, you would hear their silent crying out, in desperation and futility.

A recent event, during one cold and snowy day, prompted me to revisit, and praise, this life altering, human expression of love – THE HELPING HAND.

If you have ever experienced a time of total isolation, you will understand my deep frustration, when, after parking my old car in the garage for the night, noticed steam pouring out from under its hood – a sure sign of -- Oh, oh. To make matters worse, it was very cold, and a heavy blanket of snow made travel very difficult. Under normal circumstances, the problems this eighty-eight year old encountered would be solved— sooner, or later, but time was of the essence. I must go to the nursing home, twice a day, to feed my ailing eighty-six year old wife her daily lunch and dinner – so, what to do?

Yes, I did, in desperation, send an e-mail to my son who lives about 50 miles from me, asking for advice about my faltering car.

I'm sure you already know, "the rest of the story."

Yes, early the next morning, I heard a commotion up on the driveway – sure enough, there, was my son, removing the deep piles of snow that had accumulated the previous days (I had been unable *to use the* shovel, because of severe back pain). After he had finished the snow removal, he checked the car, and added antifreeze to the radiator cooling system; he then went to the nursing home to give his mom – *a helping hand*.

There are many wonderful gifts that are given and received
in this world; *but the most precious gifts of all:*

Are the love and friendship, of family and friends;

Who unhesitatingly offer --

THE LOVE --- OF A HELPING HAND.

A LETTER

Isn't it strange? Isn't it strange that the simple task of writing a letter can be torture for some folks, and a blessing, for others? Do you think it's the result of something in our genes? I suppose we will never know for a certainly; but, for better or worse, we will, all of us, write a bunch of letters in our lifetime. And, there is one thing, for sure; the letter is a permanent record of our thought process` at the time of inscribing, and reveals just a smidgeon of our DNA – the letter is a unique *re*flection of `who we are`.

It is an obvious fact that there are a `zillion` reasons for writing a letter, but the most rewarding, and treasured letter, is the one with `heart` (the one with love and caring). No, I'm not referring, necessarily, to carnal love; I'm referring to the `love to make a life` – just a little bit happier, and better, for someone. Ah, now we have the reason why I have embarked on this `tale of pr*os*e`, titled, "A Letter".

In the following paragraphs, I will write a letter, to my now adult granddaughters, who seem to be confused, uncertain and are struggling with the age old questions: "What is my future; what am I to do next? Or, as it has been said by so many, "I've been trying to decide what to do with myself when I grow up; and then sighing, in frustration, "Growing up is harder than I thought it would be". Yes, my granddaughters had arrived to a stage of life, when there are more questions than answers. Perhaps, Grandpa's (G'pa's) Letter will be of some help to her.

A Letter

My dear granddaughter, when I read your comments concerning the uncertainties of life, and the realization that the difficulties "of growing up," can pose some very unsettling dilemmas; I remember thinking, "gosh, those are the same frustrating, frightening moments that a young man (whom I knew intimately) had; he struggled mightily with those very same worrisome issues, so many years ago. I remember how he agonized with the same unsettling questions about life: what direction and pathway he was to follow in life; would he ever find love; was there a God; and, above all, would girls like him? Yes, those were some of the fearsome questions that the young man heroically battled, seemingly forever. But, he continued on with his life, filled with hope, openness, and "I will do the best that I am able to do for myself – and, for others".

Having encountered all the confusing and unsettling questions posed during `growing-up`, I had irritably asked the question, "How is it, that we, as a human race, have no control over our futures, or what we do in life; why can't we assert ourselves and say `enough, ` it's my life, I ought to be able to determine the direction and pathway, I will follow"!

But, alas, I eventually realized, that they (my heartfelt questions about life) were unanswerable. I soon understood that we do what we do -- it's our destiny! I then asked myself the question. "What then; what is one to do in life, how does one decide?" The answer is really mysterious (unanswerable), but it soon became obvious, that I, and I, alone, must find a solution before it is too late. I, mercifully, determined that the surest way of finding the answer is to know, and understand myself, and then, do the best that can be done to succeed – and thus, *feel good about who I am, as a person*. IT IS ONLY WHEN A PERSON IS COMFORTABLE FROM WITHIN, THAT IT IS POSSIBLE TO EXUDE HAPPINESS – AND LOVE, FOR ONESELF, AND OTHERS. So you see, my dear, life is like a puzzle that has many unfamiliar twists and curves. It may take some doing, but with patience, perseverance, courage, and a touch of serendipity (a little luck, never hurt anybody), will it be possible to find, and follow, a beautiful rainbow, leading to a happy, contented life.

Interestingly enough, although destiny appears to be our guiding light in life, it appears that when it's all said and done most of us are able to say "Heck, I'm kind of proud of what I did in life; after all, what else could I have done better"? Well. I've given you the thoughts of an old man – just thoughts.

My love,
G'pa

A PICTURE

How many of us have taken a picture of a happy event, then put it away someplace for safe keeping? And, alas, how many of us have forgotten about it, and even worse, forgotten where the heck that safe haven was?

A recent invitation for dinner, remarkably, brought back many poignant memories, and yes, even to the location of a special picture that had been taken many years ago. No, this was not an invitation for just any dinner; it was a very special dinner, in a very special place.

Although the meal was delicious and appreciated, it was the home and love that permeated it that brought back my joyous thoughts. The host and hostess for this memorable event were my granddaughter Dana and her husband Mike and the location for the affair **was their first home.**

They, as most young home owners, were proud of their first, new domicile and were engaged in improving and changing things around to suit their needs. It was obvious that their efforts were not considered work; it was a labor of love.

It was this occasion that brought back to me fond memories of a little five-year-old girl who, many years ago, helped me make a snowman during a very cold and snowy winter day. Although she, her twin sister, Laura and I had many fun times during those early years, the snowman that we constructed the year that they were five, stands out above the rest.

If you think that our snowman was a masterpiece that would have made Michelangelo jealous, think again. Actually, it was the skinniest, sorriest, most pathetic and downright awful snowman ever created. *It was beautiful!!!* It was so magnificent that someone had taken a picture if it, and worse, the picture included me and the girls. Since I was photographed with that forgettable creation, I would be forever linked to it. There is no way I can disavow responsibility. I was caught red-handed! Oh, the pain!

But you know, now after these many years, I'm glad that someone took that picture. In fact, I kind of like it. Oh, it's still a pathetic sight, to be sure, but what beautiful memories it has showered on me.

I wish there were a thousand more pathetic, beautiful pictures like it!!

G'pa with Laura & Dana (Twins --5 years old)

G'pa with Laura and Dana
Year - 2015

PS,

Ah, yes, my prayers have been answered.

G'pa

A TERRIFYING EVENING

I don't know how many people have experienced a life threatening event in their lives, but I am sure it is a vast number; especially if you consider the many wars, and other Government horrors perpetrated on their own citizens. But the brain numbing, horrifying event that I experienced one night had nothing to do with wars or any other violent situation; my life changing experience occurred when I was at peace with the world, and was enjoying a cool evening walk along a well-known path at a mountain resort. The walking and running paths at the resort were well kept, and were touted to be safe (day or night), because great care had been taken to ensure that there would not be worrisome attacks from wild animals, or other predators.

In order to properly tell my story, I must tell you the topography of the well thought-out locations of the various pathways, because it was the pathway positions to one another that possibly saved my life.

The pathways were designed to provide different panoramic views, and to give various degrees of exercise to persons of all ages and abilities. Some pathways were more perpendicular in length than others, and some provided a more horizontal, longer and level stretches, for the less athletic outdoorsman; but all the pathways were situated close enough to each other so that, if needed, emergency help could quickly be obtained.

I will now continue my harrowing story, but forgive me if I falter at times.

My decision to take an evening walk by myself was unusual by itself because, being of advanced age I am usually accompanied by my wife, or one of my children, to help me if I falter due to a medical mishap. But, it was a pleasant evening and for some unknown reason, I just wanted to be by myself for a while. I did take along my smartphone just in case of an emergency, or if I wanted to take a picture of something. *The decision to take along my smartphone was prescient – it saved my life!*

It was a warm lovely evening, not a cloud in the sky, and the aroma of forest and wild flowers made for a perfect time to be outdoors. I decided to walk along a fairly long, level pathway that didn't appear to be crowded. I had been walking slowly for about a half-mile, while observing the birds and numerous rabbits and squirrels, when I notice a well-dressed, pleasant looking gentleman approaching me. As he came closer, he nodded and waved his hand as if to say "hello". When he was about to pass me, he seemed to be scrutinizing me in a manner that sent shivers down my spine; I was relieved when he passed me. I then picked up my walking pace because somehow I sensed danger, and wanted to get as far away from him as possible.

After I had walked a few hundred feet without looking back, I stopped and looked back to see if he was gone. It was then that I knew that my worst fears were realized, he had stopped a few hundred feet from me, and with a half - smile, slowly began walking toward me; I knew then what his intentions were. Strangely, although I had fear, I remained clear headed and considered my options. I knew I couldn't outrun, or fight him successfully – so what to do? It was then that I saw him holding a cord of cloth, or wire that was tied on each end to small pieces of wood – IT WAS A GARROTTE! – He was going to strangle me!

As he slowly approached me, I thought about screaming for help, but even if there were people around, I knew they couldn't come in time to save me. I did hear voices that seem to come from a parallel path that was several hundred feet below me, however.

When he came to within 50 feet of me, he stopped, stared at me with a blank expression, grasping firmly the cord's wooden handles, and slowly came toward me. It was then that I knew I was going to die if I didn't do something quickly. Although I was shaking and fearful, I quickly reached into my pocket, grasped my smartphone, and almost simultaneously, pointed it at him, took his picture, and threw that camera over the embankment to the path below to where I thought I had heard voices. I then shouted as loud as I could, that the camera had the picture of the man who killed me.

I then looked at the man and asked him to spare me. I threw my wallet toward him, and said "If you kill me, they will catch you because I sent your picture to a friend, and I also threw the camera to the people on the path below." My only hope was that my would-be killer was sane and understood the meaning of my actions.

After I had pleaded with him to spare my life, the man stopped his advance toward me, and seemed to be confused. He didn't say a word, or move, for the longest time; he then slowly, relaxed his grips on the garrotte that he had held in his hands, turned, and walked slowly away.

I am unable to tell you "the rest of the story;" because --- thankfully,

I woke up –

It was -- a bad dream!

Thank god!

It was just a bad dream!!

BE PATIENT, BE PATIENT!

How many times have you heard the aphorism, "Be patient," in your life time? It seems that we all know what 'Be patient' means, right? But, do we? Sometime words have several meanings that can be confusing and even worrisome at times. Consider: synonyms of the word "patient," can oft'time lead us astray; words in the dictionary such as: easy-going, persevering, tolerant, long- suffering, and enduring are also listed under the word patient -- in addition to MY MEANING of the word patient – i.e. 'to be *capable of waiting'*. And finally, I guess the word 'patient' could even mean *'somebody given medical treatment'!* Well, I guess you know by now what I am trying to say – it's a tough world – Charlie Brown.

So it seems that the word, patient, could simply imply that a patient person is one who is capable of waiting--- or --- maybe not.

What, you might ask, is the purpose of my even bringing up the subject of being patient, in the first place? You probably won't believe me, but the subject of being patient, cropped up during a fun day of fishing with my friend Lon. Let me explain.

Normally, when fishing, I manage the motor, and fishing boat because I know the lake very well, since I had fished the lake for over 40 years, so naturally I was able to move about the lake quickly, and knew the various "Honey holes". So, every time we tried a new fishing area, I would say, after a few casts, "Ok, let's go, there are no fish here!" MY friend would then shout "Be patient be patient!" Each time I decided to go to another area, after a few casts, he would sigh, and say -- be patient, BE PATIENT.

After fishing a couple of hours (by the way, we soon found an area of the lake where we did catch a bunch of fish), we were having a cup of coffee and resting (from catching so many fish), when he sadly lamented, "you know Doc, I have lost some very good friends lately, why did they have to go, and why am I still here? I slowly turned around to face him, and smilingly said, "Lon, BE PATIENT -- BE PATIENT"

Now after many years, I am happy to report that Lon is still being patient; and yes, we still remember that wonderful day of fishing, and laugh about that 'Be Patient', conversation.

Now, with your kind permission, I will *patiently* continue.

What about the word, 'Love'? Do we always think of the word love, in a *loving* way? Well, the answer is: Yes, no, maybe, possibly --- humnn. Since there is some question about what the word Love implies, we will consult the fountain of knowledge, of the written-language – "the dictionary". It seems that all of the modern dictionaries agree that the word love can be expressed in many "lovely" ways. Words such as: darling, dear, sweetheart adoration, devotion, and even addiction (as, I can't break-away from – it, her) etc... So, to sum it up, love refers to a variety of different feelings, states and attitudes that range from interpersonal affections (I love my mother) or, (I loved that meal), to just an expression of, (yeah, I like it!).

If love, so loves, why is there discrepancy of meaning; is it possible that the word love is not always loveable? Consider: is the statement "I'd love to punch him in the nose" loveable? Maybe the punch in the nose was meant to be just a "Love" tap on the nose, who knows? How about the inquisition statement "I sure would love to know where he goes every night". -- Love? -- Maybe!

To sum up this feckless discussion, I will give you MY definition of the word, LOVE.

Love is caring!

PS

Caring, as in sincerely caring, that the person or persons of your affection are happy, healthy, warm, safe, well fed and prospering.

BIRDS, BIRDS, BIRDS

Sometimes, there are so many of them, that you can't see them.

No, I'm not talking about those horrible little, biting creatures, the 'no- seeums ', I'm referring to the ubiquitous birds, the Gulls. Oh, I know, you will knowingly retort that gulls --- are seagulls, so how would a landlubber know about gulls, anyway? Well it's true that I am not a seafaring man, but I do live near a small inland 'Pond' that we call a lake. It is also true that we, non-sailors, use the term "seagull" when we refer to gulls, but the scientific bird community refers to gulls, yes, -- as Gulls. You must know that these same birds, that are usually seen around oceans and lakes, are seen – *everywhere*. Gulls can be seen anyplace that "loose" food is found. It isn't unusual to see hundreds of gulls at picnics grounds, amusement parks, playgrounds, and, also, ON SMALL PONDS.

Now, my story, about Birds – the Gulls.

But, what is a Gull? A Gull is a sleek, moderate sized, web-footed, white and gray bird with a yellow or red beak. It can be found, and is native to, North America and Europe.

Gulls are aggressive, and opportunistic eating machines (aren't we all). It seems that Gulls have an elaborate, sophisticated communication network; how else would it be possible for them to all appear, within seconds, when there is food to be had? It isn't uncommon to see "literally hundreds" of them appear the moment "loose food" is found. Such was the case, the other day, when I was watching a couple of gulls flying low over the shallow water of our bay, and then, repeatedly dive into the water; they had found their "honey hole"(shallow water loaded with minnows)! Apparently, they, the two "Gull scouts," knew there would be easy prey in our small lake, in Northeast Ohio, because in late fall, the lake water is lowered to protect the shoreline and docks from the winter ice and snow. It seemed, that within minutes, the alarm had been sounded; suddenly, the sky was filled with a frantically flying, and diving, white clouds of white and grey shadows, into the water – the minnows were doomed!

The late fall, and winter months, are not usually considered prime weather months for most lakeside residents but, as is usually the case in life, – there are "trade-offs". If one is able to withstand a little cold, and solitude, Mother Nature will, at times, richly reward you with sights and beauty, beyond measure – and so it was this year. She blessed us with a trilogy of sights and sounds that she, and only she, could conjure up. She sent to us, in November, a beautiful Swan; hundreds of small, mighty, and so very beautiful, Buffleheads. And, lastly, for an encore, there appeared a bevy of exquisitely carved, graceful Gulls, replete with their noisy salutations, and wild acrobatic maneuvers.

So, you see, we often will encounter beauty, and wonderful moments, when least expected, and when it seems our lives are devoid of purpose and humor. The birds, whether in summer or winter, are destined to enrich our lives.

All that is required is the calmness of spirit, and the ability to appreciate the bounties of nature that surround us.

PS,
The Bufflehead,

We first noticed them in our bay because of their distinctive white cheek patches. The male is largely white with a black back and a black head with a greenish, purple gloss; the female is all dark with a white cheek and wing patch.

The birds are fast fliers (one of the fastest of all waterfowl). The male has a squeaky whistle and the female calls with a soft hoarse quack. No noise, however, is made in flight. They breed in Alaska and east to western Quebec and south to the mountains of Washington and Montana. They winter in the southern United States on the Gulf coast, northern Florida, Mississippi, and New Mexico; Southern West coast, and Atlantic coasts.

BRAIN, BRAWN OR, SKILL

What if I asked you an interesting question that at first blush would seem to be a `no-brainer` (easy to answer)? What if I asked the question "Which of the most often played sports played today, requires the most `brain power? ` Ah, maybe it isn't so easy a question to answer, after all!

The question that was queried might be somewhat easier to answer if the sport were a `game` like, chess (if chess can be considered a sport); but, what if we considered the semi-violent – violent sport, such as football? Would you, without thinking, say "heck no, not football, it is purely a game of mayhem; all they do is hit each other, and cause as much pain as they can on their opponents. It is simply a game of brawn (muscle), against brawn." I suppose that assessment is true to some degree, but does the game require, at least, the same `brain power` that is required in baseball, soccer, golf, badminton, lacrosse, or tiddlywink? Did I say TIDDLYWINK? No matter, I'll continue.

It is of interest that games such as golf, badminton, lacrosse and baseball etc., all require basic intelligence, but not superior intelligence; but they do require `special skills` to be successful. The superior golfer must have, above-normal coordination, vision, and nervous system, so that it is possible to strike the golf ball precisely and adequately. In other words, must have – SKILL, plus a normal nervous system, and muscular capabilities. And, so too, is it so, for most other competitive sports. And, yes, even the game of tiddlywinks requires superior skills to `squop` an opponent's `wink`.

THE GAME OF TIDDYWINKS

Tiddlywinks is a competitive game involving four colours of winks. Each player controls the winks of a colour, the colours being blue, green, red and yellow. Red and blue are always partners against green and yellow. There are six winks of each colour, which begin the game in the corners of a felt mat measuring 6 feet by 3 feet. This mat is ordinarily placed on a table, and a pot is placed at its centre. There are two primary methods of play with the four colors of winks: a pairs game, and a singles game. The pairs game involves four players, playing in partnerships, with each winker playing a single color. The singles game involves a single winker playing against another single winker, each playing two colors of winks in alternation.

The players take turns, and there are two basic aims: to cover (or *squop*) opponent winks, and to get one's own winks into the pot. As in <u>pool</u> or <u>snooker</u>, if a player pots a wink of his own colour, then he is entitled to an extra shot, and this enables a skilled player to pot all of his winks in one turn. The point of squopping, which is the key element distinguishing the adult game from the child's game (though recognized in even the earliest rules from 1890), is that a wink that is covered (even partially) may not be played by its owner. The wink on top may be played, though, and sophisticated play involves shots manipulating large piles of winks.

The game ends in one of two ways: either all the winks of one colour are potted (a *pot-out*), or play continues up to a specified time limit (usually 25 minutes), after which each colour has a further five turns. Then a scoring system is used to rank the players, based on the numbers of potted and unsquopped winks of each colour.

Wikipedia

Now where was I? Oh, yes, the game of football.

To be sure, football is, by all standards, a brutal game of `hurt` and violence. It is a game played by brawn, against brawn, and is not generally considered a "brainy" game. It is true that many players are intelligent, and `smart`, but normal, everyday smarts, is the rule. So, it can be said, that football is a game of skill, at times, and brawn – all the time.

Do you remember the original question? It was:

"Which of the most often played sports, today, requires the most `brain power?` Ah, maybe it isn't so easy a question to answer after all!

And the answer – is football – in my opinion. When I asked the question, "What sport requires the most brain power, I stated that if the game were chess, it would be a no-brainer." **Well, there you have it; it is football, no question; because, you see, football is a game of chess** that is played on a gigantic board – a field that is 100 yards in length. The football `chess players` (guards, tackles, linemen), etc., replace the King, rooks, knights, and pawns, etc. on **the** chess board (64 squares of various sizes). Both, football and chess players require considerable Brain power (*offensive and defensive coordinators, mostly*) who are responsible for placing various players to their proper positions. Although most all players have normal to above normal aptitude, and, all have mostly similar physical prowess (with some exceptions, more or less); **it is the coordinators mental abilities, and diligent research, that ultimately decides who wins, or who loses, the game.**

To summarize: The game of football requires much more planning, much more physical prowess and skill, than most other competitive sport games. In essence, **most football games are won, long before the game is played,** if, due diligence to detail had been exercised by the team's offensive and defensive coordinators; but, needless to say, unforeseen events, or environment variants from the expected norm, may also affect the outcome of a contest.

Aphorism:

Use the brain, to avoid pain

Is, the name of the game!

Tiddywinks anyone?

CHARITY

Whenever I hear the word `Charity, ` my head and heart`, are filled with various emotions that confuse me, and causes me to question how the word -- `Charity,` relates to me; and to wonder how one determines where there is true need? Oh, I know, charity means `giving` (whether of one's self, or of one's possessions), but isn't it so much more than that? Yes, *of course;* `charity ` is a fundamental human emotion that is deeply embedded, and tightly woven into the very fabric of our humanity. Without charity, there wouldn't, or couldn't, be a viable existence of any living thing. Think for a moment, could there be a livable world if `help`, `aid`, `assistance`, `gifts`, `donations`, `offerings` -- or, `handouts,` were non-existent? Would it be possible for us to stand alone in a world that is brimming with mishaps that are awaiting us at every turn of our lives, if it were not for charities' benevolence and love? I think not!

Ah, but beware, many wolves abound in sheep's clothing!

It is an obvious fact that `charity` is multidimensional in scope (latitude). It is one thing to give help to an unfortunate friend, or stranger who is in need of financial or physical help, but unfortunately, there are many misfits who falsely, or criminally, abuse the kind-loving intent of their benefactors; and thusly, cast a dark cloud over mankind's most noble virtue -- charity.

Unhappily, as is so often the case in human entanglements (relationships), there are no absolutes (rules, solutions); the very act of giving (Charity) may not achieve its intended goal. When a recipient of a charity becomes complacent (contented) with being helped even when that assistance is no longer truly needed --- degradation of spirit, ambition, and loss of self-respect, often results. **Dependency on others is a demoralizing taskmaster, and often creates a featureless burden on society.** *It is an obvious fact, that it would be much better if charity (help) were offered* **along** *with other helpful resources that would enable the recipients to help themselves; then, there would be no losers, or loss of self-respect.*

From the earliest of times, human benevolence (kindness - charity) has existed in various cultures and societies of the world. In Christian theology, charity is the greatest of the three theological virtues (Faith, Hope, Charity), and is equated to love.

Lov (CHESED) is a Hebrew word meaning loving-kindness, and is central to Jewish ethics and theology. There are some religious factions that consider charity to be just a passion, i.e. `benevolent giving`, rather than a virtue; others, such as the Roman Catholics, consider charity a virtue -- `we love God above all things for his sake, and our neighbors as ourselves for the love of God`.

The Hindu scriptures speak of Dāna -- `giving to those in distress`; "No friend is he who to his friend and comrade who comes imploring food will offer nothing". And, remarkably, *"**The foolish man who wins food with fruitless labour, that food -- I speak the truth -- shall be his ruin".*** (Hindu Book 10, Hymn117) *yH*

So, yes, it appears that charity, whether it is considered to be a passion, sacred duty (need), or simply an act of kindness (passion) --

Is deeply engrained in the human genome (DNA).

The aphorisms:

THERE, BUT FOR THE GRACE OF GOD, GO I DO UNTO OTHERS, AS YOU WOULD HAVE THEM DO UNTO YOU ---

Is the true essence (soul) of Charity.

CONGRATULATIONS

What a wonderful word is `congratulations`. There is no doubt about it; it implies "good things" were done. The person receiving the accolade is happy, and the pronouncer is happy for him, or her – WHAT A HAPPY WORD. It would seem that since it infers that someone did something `special`, one would hear the word more often than it is. Surely, `good things` are being done all around us, and would merit a congratulary nod, or at least, one of the congratulatory synonyms such as: Hats off; cheers; well done, or even, `nice one`!

It's true, that the word, congratulations, is quite often used in some circles, to bolster self-esteem, even though the compliment really wasn't for something above the norm; e.g. what parent hasn't showered a child with praise for accomplishing the monumental feat of being potty trained, or of standing, and walking for the first time? WAIT, now that I think about it, THEY REALLY SHOULD EARN PRAISE – a big congratulation is in order; consider – *everyone* is a winner with those accomplishments.

So, all well and good, if you do something "special", and if that something special is thought to be -- well, special, it would be reasonable to expect a compliment, or at least, a "well done", or "hats off to you". But, what if *you think you* did something special, and alas, no one seemed to notice, or care, that you had put enormous effort and love in your accomplishment – what then? It may be that what you think is worthwhile, is just mediocre, or worse; but what the heck, somehow, or other, your effort ought to account for something, and warrant at least a – "good effort" acknowledgement—don't you think?

There have been many accounts of "good stuff" having been ignored and forgotten for long periods of time (much to the consternation, and anguish of the creator), only to be "discovered" by future generations, and praised as a "jewel of the past". A particularly sad instance occurred for a gifted Author, who had created a book of such beauty, that it belatedly won a Pulitzer award-- after his death. The poor fellow had killed himself after he was ridiculed by his mother, who told him that he was wasting his time writing drivel.

I guess there are many reasons why an accomplishment (good or bad) can slide innocently, and sometimes, not so innocently, under the radar screen. It would seem that emotions, personality, jealousy, envy, and circumstance might also play an integral role, and thus obviate the need for accolades (congratulations). Ah, yes, the heavy burden of human frailties!

I hasten to add, that oft'time, the failure to recognize, and acknowledge a work of art, or other quality endeavor by an individual, may simply be an innocent human foible that we all are heir to -- we forget, or are unaware of its importance.

It is true, as we have discussed, there are many reasons why we sometimes fail to honor, or at least acknowledge someone's efforts by at least, shouting, a hearty "CONGRATULATIONS", but probably the most common reason is that there are too many 'happenings' in our lives that, at times, dulls our senses to the present reality. William Wordsworth's wise assessment "The world is too much with us," is so very true. We are inundated with too much "stuff" on a daily basis, so we tend to procrastinate, and make a mental note to "do it later, when I have more time"--

Alas, a time, that never arrives!

Now, I will tell you why I have decided to write about a subject that has haunted me for many years. It is a confession that I thought I would never make; I, in my innocence, did not offer a sincere congratulation to a friend who had sent to me his treasure, his recently Published Book! In my defense, I did *belatedly* offer him my congratulations, but the hurt was sustained -- no amount of repentance, or apology would ameliorate his pain.

PS,
The aphorism, "Do unto others, as you would have them do unto you."

SOMETHING TO THINK ABOUT!

CRYING OUT IN THE WILDERNESS

I wonder how many of us have ever heard a *lonely* cry emanating from the vast, wild world (the wilderness) that surrounds us. I wonder how we, as a society, would respond when we experience such an unexpected event. Do we stop briefly, and then decide it is just one of 'those things' that happens, and continue on with our lives? Or, would we stop and question why, and whence, the cry had been sounded. I suppose the answer would be appropriate to the circumstance; depending on time, place, and whether it sounded serious, and/ or if it required prompt response and attention...

But, what if I reminded you (I'm sure we all are aware) that there are endless calls 'from the wilderness' that often cannot be heard; but, all one need do, is to take the time to *look* closely, to *see* the *silent* cries of our fellow-man. Their cries can be seen in their hollow eyes; their cries can be seen in their demeanor, and tone of voice. But sadly, the loudness of their voices had been quietened; because, there is no longer hope that help would be forthcoming – what will be, will be –God help me!

For many years, as a practicing medical physician, I had heard thousands of loud cries from the wilderness, and yes, many, many silent cries, as well; there were cries of joy, despair, pain and futility. Happily, many of the cries for help were satisfactorily answered, and even the unanswerable ones, were at least attended to, and a conclusion reached – good or bad.

At times, it seems that everything is just `plain rotten` with the world. No matter what you do, there always seems to be a problem! My sister, who is 90-years old, has a 90 year-old girl friend who is constantly saying "It's always something, it's always something." Yes, she is right; it's always something! *But, sometimes it's good, that, `there IS always something`.*

The other day, I went to the nursing home (as I always do, twice a day) to feed my wife lunch and supper, because she has Alzheimer's disease. That particular day, an elderly, sad-appearing woman was seated at our table. I mention the fact that it's "our table" because we usually eat there, and it is positioned in such a way that it makes it easier for me to help my wife with her meals. So, yes, ` it's always something` -- I didn't want her to be sitting at `MY table`! So, somewhat coldly, I asked her "How are you doing?" She responded with a voice, so soft and gentle, that I emotionally melted, and felt ashamed that I had ever thought that she didn't belong, "at my table". She had gently answered "I'm fine, thank you."

Following our "introduction", I, we, talked about our lives, families and life- situations. I learned that she had reached the age of 93; had been in the nursing home for five years; has a family, but "they are all in Florida". When I asked her why she didn't go to Florida so that she would have a family near-by she sighed, and said "They come sometimes, but I have friends here." – Her crying in the wilderness had ceased. She had accepted, and was at peace, with her dilemma – "what will be, will be"!

She will *always* be welcome, to sit at MY table.

Sometimes, the loudest cry from the 'wilderness,' is the silence etched in print. Not too long ago, an old man died in the geriatric ward of a nursing home in North Plate, Nebraska. When he died, it was believed that he had left nothing of value – until they found a poem that he had written, titled "A Crabby Old man." It is a simple, eloquent, poignant, silent cry from *the* wilderness that bespeaks volumes about the true essence of humanity – and, of the agony of defeat. It is a classic example of a lost Soul crying out silently in the wilderness, with a poem, of his past, present, and lost life, and pleading to be heard; in this, the final paragraph of his poem, "A CRABBY OLD MAN".:

"I think of the years, all too few --- gone too fast

And accept the stark fact --- that nothing can last

So, open your eyes, people --- open and see

Not a crabby old man --- look closer --- see me!!

Yes, how many of us have heard the cry of a lost soul ---

CRYING OUT, IN THE WILDERNESS!!

The silence is deafening.

EDUCATION

A very interesting question was posed of me the other day, but I really didn't know how to answer it.; the question -- "What is education" Oh, sure, I know that the dictionaries tell us that education is a learning, schooling, or training discipline, but, truly, what is education? How would I best explain to a novice, in a few easily understood words, the true meaning of the word --EDUCATION? I suppose I could glibly tell him education (learning) would make him smart; or, I could tell him he will learn something new; or I could tell him learning will make him lots of money; and, of course, all the answers, would/could be true -- but did I really tell him what an education is? I think not! If all my preceding answers are essentially true, then what else need be said? Is there a definition that -- one -- fits all? Yes, of course, the answer is so obvious, that it is almost silly. A very wise aphorism, concerning the brain, says it all "USE IT, OR, LOSE IT." **There cannot be `education, 'without some process or input that makes our brains think!** *Thinking* (thoughtful, intelligent), makes it ALL POSSIBLE. The training process involved in teaching our brains to think (education), is a life-long endeavor. Aye, now we have come to the reason for this discussion of --

Why do we need an `education`?

Consider a moment; how could we exist in our uncompromising world, without the ability to think, and to make decisions that safely guide our lives and good fortunes. Would we be able to discern right from wrong, or anticipate, and plan future enterprises without THE ABILITY TO REASON, AND DISERN RIGHT FROM WRONG-- no, we would be helpless globs of protoplasm oozing in aimless infinity. *It is the wealth of past influences, school education (reading, writing, and `rithmatic), `and the many other experiences in our lives, that have influenced, and sharpened our brain-power -- **to think.***

So, if education is a multifaceted endeavor that is so much more than `going to school` -- why bother, why don't we just skip school, and just do whatever makes us happy (at least for the moment)? It is true that there are many examples of individuals having wonderful successful lives without formal 'schooling' but, if you look closely, you would find that the majority of them had to endure many difficulties, and had to attend the 'down to earth' educational institution of higher learning -- ` the college of Hard Knocks'. While it is true that the 'Hard Knocks' college produces many successes, the vast majority, for one reason or another, falter along life's difficult pathways. It is noteworthy, that the level of 'thinking' (education) of the Hard Knocks' college graduates is at high levels, but too often, due to the lack of direction and monitoring, success is aborted, and leads to misfortune and failure.

It should be noted at this time, that although there are countless number of influences that affect us, and cause us to think, and thereby 'sharpen' our brain power, there are limiting factors that are often beyond our control. It is a biological fact, that not all brains are equal in the ability to think; conversely, it is also a biological fact that a very small segment of all human brains are endowed by DNA, that have superior power of thought (intelligence) -- the so called, Mensa -- the high IQ society. I hasten to add, that all the rest of us 'normal brains' have more than enough *potential* brain power to 'think' great thoughts -- <u>if</u> only, we would avail ourselves more, of the marvelous gift given to us at birth -- our innate potential of thought.

There is an old German saying that is, oh, so true, for most of us.

"OLD TOO SOON, SCHMART TOO LATE"

FYI

Mensa is a high IQ society that is composed of individuals of all ages, and come from more than 100 countries from around the world. The only requirement for membership is to score within the upper 2% in the intelligence tests given to the general population. The membership is open to all comers, race, creed, or persuasion. The test given to qualify for membership is open to all who wish to take it.

The word Mensa comes from the Latin word meaning `table`.

Now, I have saved the best, for last:

The question of whether it is possible to grow new brain cells, has been argued for many years --pros and cons. Then, in the mid 1960's research had suggested, that yes, new cells are being made; and now, the year 2015, it has been shown that new cells are being made in certain parts of the brain -- and more remarkably, studies have demonstrated that the very act, of the learning process, itself, is associated with neuronal survival.

So, listen carefully, all you lazy brain lovers --

USE IT, OR LOSE IT

EXCUSES

I'll bet the title of this exercise in futility, (writing a short story about excuses), will cause a little twinge of remorse in all of us who see the word 'excuses', and then sheepishly will look around to see if anybody is looking at us. Not so?

The question "why the heck are you writing about EXCUSES, anyway? Well, the only possible excuse I can give for writing about excuses -- is -- I HAVE no excuse. Well, to be honest, my only excuse is that I couldn't think of a darn thing to write about, without making an excuse. I'll bet there are a whole bunch of folks who are reading this feckless narrative and are reassuring themselves that they're not guilty of making excuses -- well, maybe, just once or twice, they might have.

Really, though, who in this world has not ever made an excuse; either deliberately, or inadvertently?

Having said all of the above, just what is 'an excuse'? If we ask the dictionary, we find that the synonyms for excuse are: reason, justification, explanation, pretext, defense, apology, plea, and, vindication. In essence, an excuse is a reason why we did, or didn't do something So, now we know that excuses are not always the 'bad guys', but are actually, in many cases, the 'good guys.' Now, I don't feel so bad about writing this nonsensical treatise, it may turn out that I am nonsensible (honest, nonsensible MEANS, *showing sound judgment).* But what is, a good guy's' excuse? Would you believe --- "I'm sorry I'm late, I had fallen into a manhole and couldn't get out until help came." I mean -- how good is that -- (bad for him) but, if it's true, it sure is an example of an honest, good excuse.

Interestingly enough, however, when one hears an excuse, we more than often think 'bad thoughts' about the person who offered the excuse.

Would you like to know what others think
about the subject, 'of excuses'?

THEN READ ON ---

Quotes from ---THE QUOTE GARDEN

Don't do what you'll have to find an excuse for. ~Proverb

Excuses are the nails used to build a house of
failure. ~Don Wilder and Bill Rechin

He who excuses himself accuses himself.
~Gabriel Meurier, *Trésor des sentences*

Several excuses are always less convincing than
one. ~Aldous Huxley, *Point Counter Point*

Maybe you don't like your job, maybe you didn't get enough sleep,
well nobody likes their job, and nobody got enough sleep. Maybe you
just had the worst day of your life, but you know, there's no escape,
there's no excuse, so just suck up and be nice. ~Ani Difranco

No one ever excused his way to success. ~Dave Del Dotto

And oftentimes excusing of a fault
Doth make the fault the worse by the excuse.
~William Shakespeare

If you don't want to do something, one excuse is
as good as another. ~Yiddish Proverb

Destiny: A tyrant's authority for crime and a fool's
excuse for failure. ~Ambrose Bierce

We are all manufacturers — some make good, others make
trouble, and still others make excuses. ~Author Unknown

Your letter of excuses has arrived. I receive the letter but do not admit the excuses except in courtesy, as when a man treads on your toes and begs your pardon — the pardon is granted, but the joint aches, especially if there is a corn upon it. ~Lord Byron

And finally,

The best day of your life is the one on which you decide your life is your own. No apologies or excuses. No one to lean on, rely on, or blame. The gift is yours — it is an amazing journey — and you alone are responsible for the quality of it. This is the day your life really begins. ~Bob Moawad

Ah, yes,

No more excuses!

FIDELITY

Isn't it remarkable how some words are used -- or, not used? It would seem to me that a word so terribly important, and critical in meaning, as the word Fidelity, would be used much more often than it is. Oh, I know, we do use the word fairly often at Christmas Time, don't we? Who hasn't heart the words `Adeste fideles` belted out at Christmas Time? No? Well, how about "O come, all ye faithful"?

I've often wondered why the word `Fidelity` is spoken so rarely in everyday conversation, when its significance, is truly the anchor of our civilization. Think of it for a moment, where would we be, as a law abiding thriving people, if faithfulness, adherence to truth, honorable discharge of obligation and observation of duty were not a reality? Certainly, the astute aphorism by A. Hamilton "the best security for the fidelity of men, is to make `interest` to coincide with duty"; that is to say, if you really like, or want, something -- you're more likely, to give it your all.

I suppose the word, fidelity, -- and its meaning --`to be true, faithful`, is most often spoken or implied when used in the context of marriage; but many commercial ventures also want the world to know that, they too, are trustworthy, and that `are there` for you. Who knows, maybe they will be.

Of course, any human relationship, whether it is a causal agreement, or a contractual obligation of great importance, the Latin word, Fidelis, i.e. `my word is my bond`, *is the sinew, that binds all honest endeavors.*

Perhaps, nowhere else in the world, is `Fidelis` more visible and important, than in the world of artistry where a modeling, or a portrait, *must* reflect the real world reality i.e. "it had better look like the real thing". In today's world, mass production of an article or structure requires absolute ` fidelity of reproduction` or, all is lost.

Having said all of the above about the fidelity, of fidelity, down-deep in my soul, I have always felt that `fidelis` (*faithfulness of purpose and principle)* would be /are, the foundations of my being. I have always believed that if you believe honestly and firmly enough -- and pursue destiny determinedly enough --- Whether I win or lose ---

I will have done my Fidelis best!

GIVING THANKS

Although it is known that peoples of the world have given thanks for plentiful harvest for many Millennia, Thanksgiving Day was first observed in the United States by the Pilgrims at Plymouth Rock, in 1620 to celebrate their first harvest. It was only much later, in 1863, that Thanksgiving Day was proclaimed a national holiday by President Abraham Lincoln.

I suppose it is very important, as a nation, to have a day designated for the express purpose of giving thanks for the many blessings that have been bestowed upon us. But, there is something that is very disquieting for me concerning the concept of having just *one day* a year, to express our profound gratitude for the many gifts of life. It seems to me that Thanksgiving should be each and every morning as we open our eyes, and witnesses the miracles that surround us; such are my thoughts concerning this approaching Thanksgiving Day. I wondered how many souls really understand the true significance and meaning of the day; other than, perhaps, a day free from work.

There were other thoughts that were troubling and not easily dismissed from my mind. How can one justify giving thanks on a personal level, and not feel sad, or even guilty, about the millions of our fellow-man all over the world who are afflicted with disease, devastated by the elements, or by the insanity of war?

My thoughts then briefly reflected back to the many past Thanksgiving Days that I have experienced. Although, somewhat clouded, I can remember giving thanks, not just for the sustenance received, but for the privilege of life itself. The times were desperate due to the Great Depression of the 30's, and personal family tragedy of the loss of our mother. I can well remember how grateful I was for the courage given to me, just to continue!

The following years away from home, and dangers of WWII were surely traumatic. However, I, my family, and our nation survived, for which I will be eternally grateful and give thanks, not for just one day a year, but every minute of my life.

And so, Thanksgiving Days will come and go. Would it not be wonderful, if *all* the people of this earth *would say a sincere thank you for the gift of life*, not just one day a year, but, every day, every minute of the year?

Perhaps, some day that will be possible!

PS

I would be remiss if I didn't say a word or two about Thanksgiving Day's favorite meal that is enjoyed by many in the United States. All one need do is mention turkey, mashed or sweet potatoes, cranberries and pumpkin pie and Thanksgiving Day, immediately comes to mind.

Speaking of cranberries, did you know that the word cranberry was originally named `crane` berry, because the plant resembled a crane?

Gratefully,
Happy Thanksgiving

GOING HOME

The other night, while helping my wife with her evening meal in the nursing home, I heard the words "I'm going home". I was shocked to hear those words because "going home," heard in the nursing home, has, more often than not, sinister implications. When I turned around to see who had spoken, I witnessed the smiling face of a well-known fellow resident, who happily waved from her wheelchair, and repeated the words "I'm goin' home". Of course, I was elated to know that she was well enough to be *really*, 'going home'.

Later that evening, I thought how wonderful it is to be able to 'go home'. I sadly realized, that 'going home' would not be possible for my wife, who is incapacitated with Alzheimer's disease and who will remain in the nursing home for an undetermined period of time. I then thought back to the time when my wife had first entered the nursing home, four years ago; and wondered, if she would ever be able to say "I'm goin home," again. I remember thinking, as I entered the nursing home at that time, that the nursing home that has become her home, will also be *my heart's home, for a long time.*

The two words, 'Going home', depending on circumstance, can be heavily laden with emotional, and spiritual feelings, and yes, can replenish, and nourish our starved for solace battered souls; and is a reminder, that a 'Home' is not just a place to be, it is a "place of safety, comfort, and love" -- it truly is, where my heart longs to be.

I remember hearing the song, "Goin' Home," many years ago, and that it had torn into my sensibilities like no other song ever had. It was in 1958 that the song "Goin' Home" sung by the Great Negro singer Paul Robeson brought home the deep anguish experienced by displaced persons. It was a spiritual prayer, and a haunting plea, to be 'free', and "Goin' Home" ---

Goin' home, goin home, I'm jes going home;

Quiet-like, some still day, I'm jes goin home.

It's not far, jes' close by,

Through an open door;

Work all done, care laid by,

Goin' to fear no more.

All the friends I knew.

Home, I'm goin' home!

It was on December 23, 1893, that the Czech Composer Antonin Dvorak composed his famous Symphony No. 9 (From the New World), Op. 95, and was performed at Carnegie Hall while visiting in America. It was in the "Largo" theme of that symphony that the words "Goin' Home" were heard. Apparently Dvorak's themes in his symphony were inspired by our American Indian, or Afro-American folk melodies, and perhaps, also, from his own Bohemian folk music.

There is no question that the words "Goin' Home," carry great emotional baggage; they embody all that we are; they scream-out "I need to belong; I need to be where I am loved, nurtured and be safe -- 'I'm goin' Home'!

Who cannot remember ever hearing "I want to go home" from a child in distress" Who cannot remember ever feeling the heartfelt desire to "Go home", when life's destiny had a downturn, and the need to "go home," was overwhelming"?

And, so, it is true that, no matter how austere, distant, or humble the home may be; we all have the need, to be "goin' home," -- because ---

Home -- is where the heart needs to be.

PS,

I remember, many years ago, that a young man of seventeen who had ventured to a faraway place to fight a war that was not of his own choosing. Although there was deep anxiety and fear experienced; there, nestled deep in his soul, harbored safely, was the knowledge that soon, God willing --

I'll be a-goin' Home

GREETINGS AND SALUTATIONS

The other day, I received the shock of my life; a young man greeted me with "Good evening Sir, nice to see you". It was a wonderful welcome (greeting) that I hadn't heard for such a long time. When I first heard it, I almost turned around to see who he was addressing, I always thought that that sort of formal greeting was reserved just for `old folks` (I am only 88 years old). But, anyway, that nice welcome made me feel kind of good inside -- it made me feel just a little special.

That evening, while reading the daily paper, I experienced a nagging feeling that I couldn't understand, so I put down my newspaper, and suddenly, realized that it was that kind, young gentleman's greeting that brought back a few memories of some greetings (salutation) of yesteryears, that had made my life just a little more tolerable and pleasant. I then decided to write a paper about how important it is to be welcomed (greeted) in such a warm and friendly way; and, while I was at it, I would revisit the way other cultures, and peoples of the world, `welcome` each other.

There is no doubt about it, a warm greeting, and a warm response, is the crème de la crème` of the civilized world. Can you imagine living in a world of no crème de la crème` greetings; i.e., living in a world of degraded sensibilities, and meanness? So, yes, it is the way peoples of the world greet each other that are a reflection of the consciousness and gentleness of the people therein. It is true that the `greetings` of a culture will, and do, change over time, but the tenor (significance) need not change with the advent of the computer, or subsequent language `up-grades`, or alas, *down-grades* ` that we now have in the English language. Now, today, we have `hi`yall, instead of Dear Sir; and `how's `it go `in`, instead of `I hope all is well with you`. But, in spite of all the abbreviations and short cuts, we (all peoples) are still extending our hand in happiness, warmth and friendship. Of course, at times, greeting a person can be accomplished not just with verbal acknowledgements; there are variations of hand, body, and facial language that are used to extend an expression of warmth and greeting to one another. In the following paragraphs, we will survey some of the world's ethnic and cultural greeting practices -- *some of which I kind of like!* It should be kept in mind that the depth and emotional content of a greeting is often dependent on previous relationships, and personal involvement.

After perusing some of our world's cultural and ethnic customs relating to their greeting practices, it became obvious that not all greetings (salutations) are `equal opportunity (impartial). It appears that the elderly, parents and royalty are, and rightly so, respected and recognized, and thus, warrant *special* greetings. For instance: in India, it is permissible to hug (male, or female), but you better not hug the grandparents; no, instead of hugging them, it is the custom to touch their feet; and in return, the grandparents will bless you, and wish you a long life, to have a speedy marriage, and enjoy many children.

The greetings in Thailand are just a trifle more complex. Instead of kissing, or offering some other form of endearment, "do' nai'" is performed, i.e. place your palms together on your chest, and slightly bow your head so that the thumbs touch your chin if the greeting is for a friend; but, when greeting a senior, touching your nose is required; and, when greeting a Monk, or a member of the Royal family, the thumbs must touch the area between the eyebrows.

There is one greeting that is commonly used by the Hindus and Indian people; it is called Namasti ji (bow to you), and is a customary greeting when people meet or depart. To perform the Namasti ji, one must have the head slightly bowed; palms touching together, and fingers pointing upward, and thumbs close to chest.

And so, as we have seen, all peoples of the world have their individual ways of greeting one another, but the implicit message, whether it be a hug, touch, the spoken word, or a sincere smile, have all the same meaning as they *gently, scream out,* -- WELCOME --

I Love to be with you --
Glad you are here!

PS,

Of course, there are some cultures that have a somewhat less intimate manner of greeting. In Iran (Arabic) kissing each other on the shoulder is acceptable; but, in other parts of Iran, the custom of kissing both cheeks, three times, is a common greeting. If you visit Papua, New Guinea you are offered a warm greeting, by "snapping knuckles". In Grenada, a greeting is tapping clenched fists; in Greece, back slapping, instead of handshaking, makes friends happy.

If you are in Guam, it is proper to put one's right knuckle against an older person's forehead. In Benin, young men often snap fingers when shaking hands. It seems that it is necessary to clap hands three times, before saying hello, if you are in Mozambique; and, in New Zeeland, the Maori Indians press noses together while closing eyes. It seems that the Zambians greet each other by gently squeezing a thumb -- I shudder to think what would happen if the squeeze was, too much -- of a squeeze; and, the Zimbabwe, show respect by doing a series of slow rhythmic handclaps.

Lastly, there is one greeting that really makes sense, and I am guilty of doing it; if I am unexpectedly, approached by someone I want to greet, but my hands are soiled, I, with apology, will extend my hand, and `hygienically`, *shake his elbow*; how is that for a friendly, friendship greeting?

I never knew greeting someone ---

could be so much fun.

HANGIN IN THERE

Many, Many months ago, I heard a figure of speech that startled me, pleased me, and tortured me; it was the response offered by a remarkable elderly woman, Mildred, to a question that I had innocently asked of her, at dinner time, when I was visiting at the nursing home. The question I had asked Mildred was "Mildred, how're you doing"? It was her answer "I'm hangin in there" that startled me, because poor Mildred, was doing everything, BUT, hangin in there. Mildred was a patient in the nursing home; she was severely debilitated with Parkinson's disease, which had frozen almost all of her extremities, so that movement for her was not only difficult, but extremely painful. So, yes, here was this brave 89 year old woman, mechanically frozen by disease, but half smilingly, telling me that she is persevering, in spite of her affliction and discomfort. Her incredibly light response was like a giant wrench twisting my very soul; it was an epiphany (a sudden experience), that awakened my joy of belonging to the Human Race.

Her response, for some unknown reason, seemed to make me feel better, and even though I knew she was suffering with a body that was tortured and twisted, she, for a brief period of time, was a vibrant whole person who was saying --- "don't look at me as a victim, look at me, and see a person; I'm persevering, don't feel sorry, I'm Ok". Yes, I did look at her, and I saw a soldier, a very wonderful, brave soldier, who was fighting a losing battle to superior malignant forces.

Amazingly, her calm response, tinged with 'idiom' humor (I'm hangin in there), was unexpected, and bitter-sweet; and it immediately seemed to lift the shroud of darkness that had enveloped her; she had been transformed into a 'knight in shining armor' who was fighting the evil 'dragon of darkness'. She had won the respect and hearts of all who knew her -- there was never a thought of pity.

The following days and weeks were a witness to a continuing struggle for her, a battle 'of wills' between 'a giant of self-defense' and her unrelenting, attacking, merciless foe. It was only a matter of time that fatigue and age, decided the fatal outcome for our valient warrior, Mildred.

Although I had not been fortunate enough to have known Mildred for a longer period of time, I felt that I knew her for 'a life time', and felt compelled, and was honored, to say good-bye to her in a manner befitting a Queen among Queens; and to wish her -- A SAD FAREWELL

My Eulogy

My dear friend, Mildred, brave soul and battle-tested warrior; you have fought an unrelenting cruel adversary, but sadly, have ultimately lost the battle for life. Yes, dear friend, you lost the battle against the dreadful odds of disease and "time" but have emerged triumphant, although bruised and bloody. You have shown that the human spirit can conquer adversity, even when heavily afflicted with a merciless disease (Parkinson's disease). You have fought the battle with courage, understanding and dignity but, alas, ultimately lost the battle when the malignant forces of illness, and the ravages of age (89 years old), became insurmountable.

My dear, allow me the privilege to use "Mildred" when addressing you, even though I have only known you for a short period of time. I remember that our first meeting was tenuous, at best. It was at a time that my wife was assigned to be your roommate in the nursing home. It was a very difficult time for us, as it must have been for you. My dear wife had been in the hospital for several days and needed rehabilitation and nursing care. But, the following days and months were pleasant (as much as can be expected). Eventually, we met your loving family, who visited frequently for meals and other events. You know, Mildred, I remember how you bravely smiled, at times, even though you didn't feel well. I will never forget your response when asked "How are you doing". Your witty response was: "I'm hanging in there!" *And so you did!*

We, all living creatures, must eventually follow the dictates of nature. We must all, at one time or another, escape our earthly bonds, and enter a sanctuary where there is eternal peace and happiness. I know that your prayers will surely be answered.

So, dear friend, I bid you a fond farewell.

May God be with you

HOME FOR CHRISTMAS

Christmas time for the Christian World, is a time for happiness, sadness, and soul searching (searching of one's motive's and life's meaning); it is a time for profound gratitude and celebration of the coming of our messenger of love, Jesus Christ. Woven within the fabric of love and happiness of the Christian celebration, is the sadness of having loved ones, and dear animal friends who are physically gone, but not forgotten, at Christmas time.

Christmas time is often thought by many to be a moment in time of each year, to reflect on past loves, and lost friends; it is Christmas card, and `letters ` time, to remind us that love, in a world that is so often devoid of compassion, is our only salvation. It is during this season of heightened spirituality, love and remembrances of lost loved ones, that miracles, and unusual events are often encountered -- and yes, even `dreams` may suddenly, vividly, and realistically be summoned.

In my dream one night, I experienced a confusing set of unusual events that I am certain were a reflection of my persistent sadness of having lost my dear feline friend of many years, PLT (Pretty Little Thing).

Permit me a few moments, to falteringly tell you, about my dream that I had witnessed one Christmas Season, a dream --- of Christmas love --

HOME FOR CHRISTMAS

I am somewhat confused as to why I experienced this dream, because I really hadn't been especially thinking about my lost little bundle of joy, my cat PLT, although every day, and, yes, every Christmas, I do think fondly of her, and remember how she loved the Christmas season with its bright multicolored Christmas tree lights, and how she loved `hiding under the tree` and batting at the tree lights. She seemed to be happier when everybody paid more attention to her; and she dearly loved the `cat nip` toys. My loving friend had died a few years ago, because of age and disease.

My dream

Although I do occasionally have dreams at night, especially when I had a tiring, or emotional day; this night, a few days before Christmas, I felt unusually relaxed, and had enjoyed an evening of pre-Christmas comradery and felicity -- all was well with the world --- I would hopefully have a pleasant nights rest, and a busy day on the morrow.

I have no idea where I had been visiting, but I think it was a nursing home, or a convalescent care center. I think it was a nursing home because I have been going daily to a nursing home for many years to help my wife who is suffering with Alzheimer's disease.

As I was leaving the building one evening, I noticed a small, pretty kitty that was trying to get into the building. She appeared ill-kept, hungry, and shivering (it was severely cold that evening). I remember thinking she looks just like my lost PLT when she was young, with her white face and white chest fur; begging to be hugged and caressed. So, as I was leaving, I activated the wall switch that automatically opens and closes the entrance door, so my little friend could enter and get warm, and maybe, a kind soul will give her something to eat.

Amazingly, when I opened my car door in the parking lot, a blur of fur flew past me into the car -- it was my little friend. She obviously was intent on going home with me. My first thought was to evict her from my car, because I had previously resolved to not ever have another feline, or any other animal `friend,` because *I could not stand the sorrow* of losing another loved animal. But, it was late, and cold, so I thought I would keep her for the night, and take her back to the nursing home the next day when I go to feed my wife her lunch. Upon reaching home, my newfound friend seemed to know that she now had a home, and quickly dashed through the door as I opened it -- **it seemed to me, for a moment, that my precious PLT had returned home -- what a wonderful Christmas it would be!**

The next morning, having slept soundly for the first time in many months, I fed my new found friend her breakfast of tuna in water, and warm milk (my PLT's favorite breakfast) -- within minutes, all the food vanished as if by magic; she was one happy and contented cat. Finally, it was time to go to feed my wife at the nursing home, and return my friend back to nature. I have to be honest, I actually though of keeping her, just for the winter months, but decided it would only hurt me more to leave her, after knowing -- and loving her, so I sadly decided against keeping her. When the time arrived to go, she had disappeared. I looked high and low, but could not find her; apparently, she had decided that she would not allow me to find her, and take her back to the misery that she had recently left. Since it was getting late and I had to hurry, I decided that I would take her back later in the day, or the following day.

The next morning, I once again fed her her breakfast, but at a little earlier time, so that I could be with her just a little longer before we were to leave. I was sitting in my TV chair in the living room having my coffee, when suddenly, a blur of fur pounced on my lap, and flung her paws high up on my chest, and looked lovingly, directly into my eyes --- *just like my dear PLT used to do.*

It was truly a wonderful Christmas dream; my beloved PLT --- WAS

HOME FOR CHRISTMAS

PS,

Dreams, dreams -- Oh, yes, we all --- must have dreams.

HOME IS WHERE THE HEART IS

Have you ever been in a `Nursing Home`? Have you ever really wanted to visit, or be a `patient` in a nursing home? If your answer is in the affirmative, I would be surprised, and alarmed, that `something` might be amiss with you. It is no surprise that most folks would prefer, and choose, a happier environment to spend either a few free moments, or the rest of their lives, elsewhere. But, with life being what it is -- a gamble, it is possible -- no, inevitable, that some of us will eventually be either, a `short term client` of a `nursing home`, or, sadly, will need to make a nursing home, -- our home, for the rest of our lives. The aphorism "there, but for the grace of God, go I" should be a truth we all understand.

Early in our lives, we blindly, and happily pursue happiness as if there was no tomorrow, we think we are invincible (especially, when we are teenagers) -- `the world is our oyster`; and, we innocently ask, what could go wrong? But, as we advance in age (and hopefully, in knowledge), we still continue to have a `blind eye` to the thought of misfortune but, at times, may be uneasily aware of `the hurt` of others -- but, mostly, --` it's everyone for themselves mentality.'

As the years swiftly pass, and we begin to notice the inevitable physical and mental transformations of aging, we do worry that "I'm getting old", and, "I hope I don't get to be as bad off, as that guy over there." Then, alas, we notice that more and more friends and neighbors seem to be getting sick and dying, or *need to be in a nursing home*; yes, finally, the truth sinks in, **we are** `getting` old --- but maybe, just maybe, "I won't need to be in a nursing home -- or worse".

Well, one needn't be a `great thinker` to know, and realize, that advancing age is fraught with danger and realize that `bad` things, do happen; -- and yes, the need for a `nursing home` looms` ever so much closer.

And, so, one day, a loved one tragically requires more assistance for their everyday needs and survival than can be physically or mentally provided, and hence, there is need for the care and caring of a `nursing home`.

I will now continue the story of the `home and heart` -- `THE ODDESY OF A NURSING HOME`.

`HOME IS WHERE THE HEART IS`

There is nothing more heartbreaking and cruel, than to have to make the decision to force a loved one to live their remaining lifetime in a nursing home; there can be no rationalization that would / could possibly ameliorate the pain and guilt of making that determination; even though it was made honestly, and was justifiably necessary.

It was at that moment, when I first entered the nursing home to see my wife that I knew the nursing home that was now her home, would also be *my heart's home*; how does one accommodate the sudden destabilization of one's life, and dreams, when that person is 88 years-old, demoralized, and physically uncertain? I suppose the answer would be the same at any age; but sadly, *it is* a crying, confusing, and, bewildering time.

It would appear, that The Supreme Curator of all creatures large and small had planned our life's final journey meticulously well; because, with the passing of time (year, after, year) of my presence, and being with her for lunch and supper on a daily basis, had helped her accept her fate, even as her Alzheimer's malady was slowly draining her body's treasures and mind.

And so, for the past many years (5 years at home, and 4 years in the nursing home), my love and caring for her has been physically, and mentally difficult, but wonderfully heartwarming for me. I know that there are many medical journal warnings, and sad reports concerning stress related outcomes for caregivers, but I honestly believe, that her need for my love, help and understanding, has for the past 9 years, kept me functional and physically active as I rapidly approach my 89th birthday.

Hopefully, there will be just a bit more time allotted to me on this earth that will allow me to fulfill my vowed commitment of long ago -- to love, care and cherish her --- Until death -- do us part.

HORNETS

TODAY, I WAS `BITTEN` BY A HORNET!

I don't know how you feel when you hear, or see, the word, `Hornet,` in print, but it sure gives me the `creeps`; it even hurts to write about this venomous, ne'er-do-well, little monster. I know, that supposedly, every creature in the world is supposed to have a purpose, or a reason for being alive but, for the life of me, I KNOW NOT WHAT IT IS. It is now early Fall, so I guess, it's the `hornet biting-season-time` of the year. I'm still not sure how the `varmints` were able to build their nest in our `night light` without detection, but now, while my friend and I were painting the deck, he was suddenly stung on his forehead. We later found a very large paper-thin hornet's nest, securely entrenched in the bowl, of my near-by night light. NOW WHAT DO I DO?

To be perfectly honest, this wasn't the first time that I have had contact with the little beasts. A couple of years ago I, innocently, was minding my own business (mowing the lawn), when I was attacked by several pugnacious, @$ %*(0^%, hornets, when I apparently came to close to their nest that was nestled in a near-by large shrub. As all "having been bitten" folks will attest, they, the hornets, show no mercy, and will chase you `half-way around the world` to get you.

It has been well documented, that being stung by a wasp can be a very painful or deadly experience. There are some folks (me included) who are extremely allergic to the wasp (hornet) toxin; but, in some extreme instances some folks will need urgent emergency treatment i.e. ice packs, adrenalin injections, and cortisone to prevent death. As luck would have it, my friend was not allergic to bee, or hornet venom, and escaped with just a little swelling and redness.

Now, back to the immediate hornet problem

I have to admit, that I handled the 'Hornet nest' situation in a totally wrong (stupid) way -- I attacked the nest with a can of 'hornet-killer' spray --- **in the 'daytime'.** Well, heck, I was MAD; I WAS DETERMINED TO GET THEM BEFORE THEY GOT ME -- I made the fatal mistake of losing my temper, and acting -- before THINKING. Any good military tactician will tell you, "look at all the possibilities, and plan your attack carefully". Yep, **I should have waited until dark** -- and THEN sprayed the nest -- when **ALL** the hornets are tucked in for the night. I soon learned, that 'haste makes waste, ' and that you should always know your enemy, before attacking.

Know your enemy

The true hornet (Vespa) is somewhat different that the other vespines (wasps) by the width of the vertex (part of head behind the eyes), and other slightly different anatomical variations. Hornets are commonly seen in Europe, Asia, North America and North East Asia. They nest in trees, shrubs, cavities of trees --- and, CAVITIES OF NIGHT LIGHTS! *As an aside, the name "hornet" is used because of their habit of building aerial nests, rather than subterranean nests*; but don't be careless, because their closely related family members, the smaller "yellow jackets," DO have subterranean nests. But -- yellow jacket, or hornet -- they are both, mean critters, and their 'stings' are -- mighty painful.

The sting of most hornets are vary, bad, bad, bad; but the sting of the Asian giant hornet, has the most deadly venom known, and is the cause of many deaths in china and Japan.

It appears that once again, chemicals reign supreme in the animal world. I'm sure we all recognize the importance of the numerous chemical compositions that make life possible for all of us; but some of those very same chemicals when in the wrong hands, -- er, in the 'vespines' stingers, can "do us in"! Fortunately, another chemical, adrenaline, is our salvation; a small amount, timely administrated, is a life-saver for most insect stings.

Why do hornets attack us?

Will wonder of wonders never cease, the hornet has its own `bugle` Alarm/attack system -- called, "the attack pheromone"; but, unlike the loud blast of a bugle belting out the `protect our colony`, or, `attack the enemy, cry ` the pheromone, is composed of three biological active chemicals that *silently*, call the hornet troops to battle. To make matters worse for their enemies, hornets and wasps, unlike their relatives the honey bees, do not die after they sting someone, because their stingers are not barbed, and therefore, are not *pulled* out of their bodies when they sting somebody -- so, they are able to sting multiple times.

Now, I will tell you, the rest of this "Hornet Biting" story.

As I stated at the onset of this story, my friend and I were painting my cottage deck, when suddenly, he was stung on the forehead. Subsequently, when we found the hornet's nest in the outside, overhead lamp fixture, I thought it would be a `piece of cake` to quickly spray the hive with my pressurized can of hornet-killer, and that would be -- it -- no more hornets. Well, I did spray the nest, and quickly moved about twenty feet away and waited to see what would happen. Sure enough, many hornets came zooming out of the hive. But, alas, it couldn't have been more than a few seconds after I had sprayed the hive, when I felt a severe pain on the inner-most portion of my left upper arm. The pain was very severe (like someone had stuck a red-hot poker in my arm). I didn't do anything about the sting, at first, because I thought it was only a superficial sting, since I had quickly swatted at the stinging hornet and, after checking my arm, I couldn't even find where I had been stung.

It wasn't until later that day that I experienced more pain, and a fair amount of swelling of my arm above the elbow. The following morning, my whole arm (above, and below the elbow) was severely swollen, and the pain was quite severe. It was two more days before most of the swelling had somewhat subsided, and I felt that I might live.

In retrospect, I did a whole bunch of wrong things, about this Hornet's nest thing. Firstly, know that the hornet is a formidable enemy, and should be approached cautiously, i.e. never spray a hive in the daytime -- always wait until night to spray the hive. Secondly, always treat the sting as an emergency, and have the proper "sting - treatments" readily available (ice, cell phone, adrenalin-auto- injector, and cortisone (oral or injector). I must confess, I waited too long before I used ice, and I couldn't find my auto-adrenalin injector, but I did take some cortisone tablets even though they wouldn't have helped me if I had experienced anaphylactic shock (allergic reaction); oral cortisone requires at least 24 hours before it would be therapeutically effective

Well, now that we know all about hornets and their habits, and how to treat hornet stings, we should now be safe --- right? ------- Wanna bet? --

See you -- in the emergency room

PS,

Pheromone,

Is a secreted or excreted chemical factor (Greek phero "to bear" and "hormone", from Ancient Greek ὁρμή "impetus") that triggers a social response in members of the same species. `Pheromones` are chemicals capable of acting outside the body of the secreting individual to impact the behavior of the receiving individual.

Wikipedia -- the free encyclopedia

HUMILITY

If you were asked the question "How does one measure the true worth (value) of an object or, of the `quality` of a man; how would you respond? The obvious unthinking answer would be, "that's easy, it's unto the eyes of the beholder" – But, is it? It is, probably true, that the value of an article of `everyday commerce` can be adequately evaluated by a trained market beholder (professional) but, how is one to determine the *true* worth of an individual. Is it possible; is there even the remotest possibility, that an impartial, scientific, accurate evaluation could be applied to encompass all the physical, mental, emotional, psychiatric etc. variable determinants inherent in all creatures?

If, indeed, there is, a starting point for evaluation of a person's worth, and if that is so, where would it be? Would you first garner as much information about the individuals life, i.e., birth pedigree, background, past exploits, accomplishments (physical, mental, professional, emotional etc.), and then add them up to compare with a predetermined `quality chart`? Ah, yes, you would have a score, but would that score represent the true *total* worth of the individual? *If the answer is in the affirmative, would you not have reservations that there might be information unbeknownst to you that might change your mind? Might there not be `shades of information` that might alter the scoring?*

There is no doubt that all the reasoning's reviewed above, concerning the quality of a person, do have merit and might in some circumstances accurately reflect the true `essence` of a person; but, hold on, there two more variables that are, or are *more* important, than all the previous attributes that have been considered; They are: What is their `*future-potential`; and, `the presence of hu*mility`!

Who has not seen a beautiful table, or a beautiful art masterpiece emerge from the substance of an average lovely tree? Who has not witnessed the transformation of a solid block of marble artfully transformed into a `Michelangelo` masterpiece? And, yes, the beautiful endowments of an individual are similar to those of a tree or a block of stone. The natural, inborn potentials of an individual are also readily available to be molded by future external forces, potentially, into a masterpiece of incredible beauty (value). It appears, then, that it is impossible to determine the true worth of a person, until "it is all said, and done". And furthermore, an even more intriguing dilemma is posed by the inevitable question -- "What if?" Certainly, there are myriads of `what if's` in our lives that could, and do, alter our life's history book.

HUMILITY!

Now that we have come to the reason for this discussion "How then, does one measure the true worth (quality) of a person"? The previous discussion mentioned the difficulties encountered when evaluating the many variables broached when determining the quality of a man, and found them to be only of modest help. So, what now? Would it be possible to simply ask a few personal question of an individual and, depending on his answers, quickly make a judgment about his `quality`; if so, what questions would be asked? Would the questions be: "How smart are you?" or, "Do you think you can do this better than anyone else? "An arrogant man would certainly proclaim I'M THE BEST, and shout that he -- IS THE GREATEST! Alas, the poor soul is so infatuated with himself, that he is unable to understand that there is always someone better, and smarter; his value and contributions to the world are sadly sequestered into a locked narcissistic (self-love, self-importance) vault, and thus, is hopelessly rendered valueless.

If, on the other hand, there is humility (unpretentiousness), he would not understand that he is what he is, and that he is no better, nor worse than anyone else; he is willing to accept limitations, and submit himself when, and if, it is appropriate, to a higher source.

This person is morally, and ethically whole –

He is praiseworthy, and of high quality.

PS,

And so it is, the value (worth) of a person cannot be determined "until the final bell is rung," and all the "what if's" that had occurred in a person's life are evaluated; humility (humble, unpretentious), is truly, a virtue of great value, when the worth of an individual is to be determined.

As an example of "from what I speak;" please allow me the pleasure of telling you the story of a humble man, and his remarkable ability to create great beauty, for beauties sake, alone; beauty that should not remain undiscovered.

This story is, thankfully, a very common example of the virtue – Humility. As is so often the case, beauty and quality of spirit, are discovered by mere chance.

This is the story of a Grandfather who, **unbeknownst** to family or friends, had created creations of great beauty, with great talent and skill. It was only because his grandson fortuitously found, and filmed, this wonderful, humble man's masterpieces, that they are now available for the world to see.

There is no need to say more.

INTEGRITY

Isn't it strange? Isn't it strange that I feel elated, subdued, and even reverent, as I embark on this story (mission) titled: **Integrity**? Why would there be such drenching emotions, or such passion evoked, when this innocent word comprised of only nine letters is mentioned? Perhaps such passionate sentiments are summoned because the word `Integrity` is, or should be, the Holy Grail, of the civilized World. It is a word (its true meaning) that, when observed, will impart a quiet joy to the beholder; because, it is understood, that there will be honesty, unity, wholeness, and a steadfast moral and ethical conduct in all future transactions. Yes, thankfully, there will now be assurance, and peace-of-mind, that whatever is encountered will transpire on a level playing field.

Perhaps, the English playwright, poet and actor, Shakespeare, had said it best in his Play, Hamlet, when the actor, Polonius, eloquently expressed the virtue of integrity:

TO THINE OWN SELF BE TRUE

This above all; to thine own self be true,

And it must follow, as the night the day,

Thou canst not then be false to any man.

Although the word, integrity, is more often used in reference to human relationships, it is certainly awfully important in all of life's endeavors. Consider: The doctor remarked, after examining a patient who had fallen, "I don't think the patient fell because of illness; no abnormal physical abnormalities were found, and the *integrity* of his nervous system was normal, therefore, look elsewhere, for the reason why the patient fell.

Needless to say, integrity in Politics is terribly important because politicians are elected to represent society. They are representatives of the people, who are expected to be honest and to do the right thing for all concerned -- they are expected to govern with INTEGRITY. Of course, integrity in other fields of endeavor such as Medicine, structural engineering, and material science is vitally important, if a society is to thrive.

Having said all of the above, it is obvious that `integrity` is the life blood of a civilization, and when there is "low integrity" there is meanness, mayhem and dissolution of the world as we know it.

But how is one to know when there is integrity -- or, alas, 'low integrity'? Well, it turns out that folks who have 'low integrity' *are the very ones* that report more dishonest behavior, and may even try to find reasons to justify that behavior. And strangely enough, they (low integrity folks) think OTHERS are more likely to commit crimes i.e. theft's; and interestingly, the "low" folks also have impulsive behaviors, and think that society should severely punish any such deviant behavior of others.

Ah, now, we have come to the interesting part of this puzzle. Would it not be disastrous for a High Teck company, or a Medical Facility to hire a person who may be of "low integrity"? Of course, persons of "low integrity" could quickly destroy a prosperous Company that had thrived as an organization of high morals i.e. integrity. *So, how do you NOT hire a person of 'low integrity"?*

Obviously, it would be helpful if there were a way to test for "Low integrity" of a new hire. Ah, yes, there is a test, "the integrity test" that is sort of like a 'reverse' psychological stimulant. *The test uses these same destructive traits in the test against the folks of "low integrity" (who have a history of deviant behavior, and who advocate harsh punishment be applied for the deviances of other people).* It appears that such tests are able to detect "false answers". If, for example, the question about devious behavior, or about their thoughts about deviances of others, *the respondents are psychologically fooled, and report some of their own past deviances, and thoughts about the deviance of others; fearing that if they do not answer truthfully, their untrue answers will reveal their own "low integrity".* **They believe that the more**

truthful they are in their answers, the higher their "integrity score will be. For some strange reason, the "low integrity individual is flimflammed (tricked, deceived) by their own naiveté (candor).

Since Integrity is a personal choice (although this may not always be true), it is hoped that most folks would realize that being honest, forthright, and have high moral and ethical standards, would profoundly benefit (soften, smoothen) their own life's journey.

PS,

On a personal note: I have lived in, and among, this 'world of people' for many, many years (would you believe - 88 years), and have spent many years attending to the 'woes' of the afflicted (as a Physician); but I honestly, have never seen, or been confronted by a truly "low integrity" (entity - person). Oh, sure, there were 'lapses' (temporary) of judgment for some, but thankfully -- there was

Integrity -- for most!

KINDNESS

There are several words in the English dictionary that bespeak of human emotions (love, hate), etc., but there are only a few that carry such deep emotions of the human condition (humanity) – as the word, KINDNESS. Kindness is *not* something that is spoken, and therefore, IS; Kindness, is a deep-rooted emotion that is keenly felt, and when given without reservation, the world becomes a warmer, loving, and safer place to be.

Kindness is an ethereal language that is remarkably understood by all Humanity – and, by all life forms. Kindness is the language that the deaf can hear; and the blind can see (Mark Twain); and, if I may add, the downtrodden understand.

But, what is kindness? Kindness is a word that encompasses many emotions. Yes, the word kindness means *compassion* (the response to help when suffering of others is encountered); kindness is sympathy "fellow-feeling," it is `feeling`, perception, and is understanding of another's distress; kindness is kindheartedness – is having and showing sympathy (and, kindness).

SO, yes, kindness – IS the culmination of our virtues (the essence of our character – moral excellence), that abides in the human soul. It is HUMANITY!

Have you ever read an account of a horrible tragedy that made you cry? I'm sure most of us have read stories that touched our hearts, and we cried (before we even had time to look around to see if someone was watching us). We cried because we have HUMANITY – (kindness, compassion, sympathy, and kindheartedness). Even the most `hardened` rogue that we can imagine, has cried out (or, at least, inwardly pleaded for help) at one time or another, when his emotions had run rampant beyond his control.

Well, I must admit that I, **too, cry** when I am overwhelmed with grief, but strangely enough, I recently cried when I read about the horror experienced by the people of Nepal, after enduring the horror of a 7.8 earthquake. I used the words `strangely enough` because I cried, not for the suffering masses, but because of an act of kindness by a local merchant; my faith in the human race was restored – and I cried the tears of happiness.

Of course, I felt terrible for the people of Nepal, but sad as it was; my thoughts were strongly geared to give the victims help and support, not just sympathy and kindness.

Now, the account of Shyam Jaiswal,

A Kathmandu, Nepal `Street fruit vendor`, Shyam Jaiswal

April 26, 2015

A short period of time after a 7.8 devastating earthquake, he said:

"This is all we have for a while, more people are coming now.

They cannot cook, so they need something they can eat raw".

"We try to help everyone, but we are not raising prices –
that would be illegal and immoral profit.

That would be wrong!"

So, yes, I cried when I read that humble man's words, and because,
I had just beheld the true meaning of kindness, compassion, sympathy,
kindheartedness – and humanity.

PS,
   "Be kind, for everyone you meet is fighting a harder battle."
   Plato

   "You cannot do a kindness too soon, for you never know how soon it will be too late."

Ralph Waldo Emerson

LIFE'S TIMELINES

It is an amazing thing, this `time` thing! It seems that everything we do in life, is monitored, and defined – by - `time`. You might legitimately ask "So what; what can we do about it"? True enough, time is -- time, and time waits for no one, but, it's also true, that if we utilize *our* `time` wisely, we can make a difference for ourselves, and others.

But, why would I talk about time, in the first place? Well, since I am very quickly approaching `THAT TIME` (since I am now nearing my 90th year on this earth (89)), I DO have a `slightly` focused viewpoint when it comes to `time`. But enough about `time`; the reason for this discussion is NOT about time, per se, but HOW, time is used in our lives, and HOW, we time our life's events.

You probably won't believe this, but a "thank you" letter from a Granddaughter revived strange emotions, and memories, of my `moments` during by-gone years. When I received her letter, I really didn't know how I should respond, or even, if, I *should* respond. But, for whatever reason, I began to think back to the many years of *my* oft'time *uncertain* passages through the years that had been allotted to me; and, strangely, I began to mentally partition segments of my life's experiences into `time periods`.

So Yes, I did respond to my granddaughter's letter, and yes, I did have special thoughts about the various time-periods of my life.

My LETTER -- TO `A FAR-AWAY-LIVING` Granddaughter

Dear Granddaughter,

Don't be amazed that I decided to write this letter; I just wanted to remind you, that I am more than just a name who sends you a yearly acknowledgement at holiday and birthday time. In addition, I also wanted to make a few observations about the comments you made in your recent `thank you letter`. You said "had a great birthday and *am excited* for my thirties." I don't know why I was stirred, but then, I tried to remember how I felt about "turning thirty, "oh, so many years ago". Actually, I think I always thought – I would ALWAYS be thirty; that is, until I unexpectedly reached my seventieth birthday year—what a shock!

The 'thirties' for me, were the 'honey' years. It was during my thirties that I had a new family, and was happily married to an Angel; and, I had, gratefully, achieved my prized goal in life of becoming a Doctor of medicine. In summary, my 'thirties' - years, were truly life-altering, happy, and rewarding years!

So my dear, you truly should be excited; your up and coming 'thirties'-years will hopefully, be your years of energy, hope, compromise, endeavor, happiness and promise.

> *The 'thirties'- years, are the pathways-years that will guide*
> *your future life's journeys. May the 'thirties'- years of your life,*
> *construct the 'road of happiness' that will carry you safe and*
> *sound through the endless maze of life's uncertainties.*

PS

There is an old German saying "old too soon, *schmart* too late" that seems to be a reality of life. Although age is not a guarantee for wisdom and good judgment, it does increase the chances that a few 'schmarts' might have been absorbed if one had a receptive mind throughout life. However, there are persons who, instead of living and learning with each succeeding year, live one year over and over again, stagnating in the process.

I have learned other truisms during my lengthy travels along the roadways and byways of life; some are harsh, but most are acceptable and just. Consider the statement "Respect the elderly." To be sure, that would be proper, but only if the sentence were completed to read "if they have earned it." Age is simply a time of life, not a prize to be exploited. There are, of course, many other sayings such as: "The world owes me nothing" and "there is no free lunch", that is true at *any* age. And, lastly, there is no doubt that advancing age does create infirmities and disabilities that require caring and kindness, but that same attentiveness, is mandated for *any* age.

It is now the year, 2015, and I am, for better or worse, eighty- eight years old. I am honestly able to affirm, that all the above aphorisms are true – and, gratefully add --- Amen!

Yes, the highway of life is still a bumpy journey but, remarkably, there are fewer "potholes" and dangerous curves that require circumvention. Perhaps the reasons why my recent travels have been less traumatic has to do with the fact that I have fewer occasions to travel far afield, and the pace of travel has been significantly curtailed.

Oh, sure, there seems to be many more rainy days lately, and the sunshine seems to be less radiant and warm. Perhaps it is nature's way of posting signposts of caution for this weary traveler's future travels.

And so, I am grateful for the opportunity to continue my journey for just a little longer. Hopefully, I will be able to help smooth the way for others who will follow me down the same potholed, bumpy -- highway of life.

LONELINESS

Loneliness is a state of mind!

To be sure, loneliness is often defined as being alone, or a state of solitude, but it truly is – a state of mind (thinking makes it so). How many times have we seen, or heard, of a person being lonely while being surrounded by people? Good examples of "loneliness- in-a- crowd" would be a soldier surrounded by many companion soldiers, or a freshman college student surrounded by fellow students. So, then, what is loneliness? Loneliness is an emotion that is all too commonly found in all animal societies; I say animal, and not human, because our four legged friends also suffer loneliness); it is a unique and multifaceted emotion suffered on a personal basis. Loneliness, therefore, is not "the being alone" that causes the damage, IT IS THE PERCEPTION of being alone. It is a mental aberration!

Having said all of the above, I must admit that there are times when I am *just plain lonely* – WHEN, **I AM** ALONE. But, I will continue.

Having outlined, and defined loneliness, what are the causes, symptoms, and consequences of such an emotional and devastating disorder?

By now, I am sure that you have said, if not shouted, "STOP," while reading this narration, "this author of `loneliness` is either `nuts`, or is "on something"!, of course, recognize the fact that being lonely can be a perfectly normal circumstance IF, you're lonely only on occasion – we all do get lonely sometimes. Consider, for a moment, the plight of a man or women who had just lost their loved one; would they not be devastated and lonely? No, the loneliness I am referring to is much deeper and unforgiving. It is the individual who has the perception (state of mind) of feeling empty, and unwanted; it is loneliness that craves human interaction, but is mentally unable to make friends. If one feels unworthy, and lacks self-confidence, would not this lack of self-esteem lead to isolation, and loneliness?

The consequences of chronic loneliness are quite severe. We have all read countless stories of loneliness leading to suicide, antisocial behavior, and alcoholism or drug addiction. But, symptoms and diseases less commonly attributed to loneliness such as: memory loss; decreased learning capacity; altered brain function; unable to sleep, and alterations of deep body metabolism, which, if untreated, may lead to premature aging, etc. So, what to do?

Oft' times, circumstances may make it near impossible to prevent loneliness. If one is injected into a milieu so austere and muted (such as in a nursing home), finding a meaningful friend or, to just find someone who will take the time to listen to what you have to say, would be a miracle. After all, all residents in the nursing home are there because of illness, disease, or some other untoward malady that had made it necessary for them to be there; friendship is a virtue they cannot afford.

It is because of my recent experiences while attending to my wife's daily needs in a nursing home, and observing the loneliness of some of the residents, that I felt compelled to revisit the sad affair, that is, loneliness.

One need not look too far afield in the nursing home, to see the awful tentacles of the 'loneliness' monster. There often can be heard the cry "Help me"; there are usually one or two residents arriving at your table to discuss the weather, or some other undiscernible topic. Many times, our mealtime audience will arrive at our table via wheelchair, and observe our every 'bite-full,' from very close quarters. Although their arrival to our table at lunch or suppertime can be exasperating at times; their need to be close to someone bespeaks loudly of their loneliness, and their need for solace.

Lastly, as always, the human race has always tried to make things better, or to "invent a better mouse trap", and so it is with, Loneliness; how can we make it a 'less lonely' world for the afflicted. But, just as most things in this world, as we have previously discussed, loneliness is a multifaceted, intricate malady, so different approaches to achieve a remedy must be researched to obtain a cure.

Certainly, if it is a "normal" lonely person, all he/she must do, is get off their duffs, and follow the aphorism "to one's self be true"; the truth that emerges will often solve the problem.

It is obvious, that if the loneliness is the result of a psychiatric, emotional, or physical condition, a remedy may be difficult to obtain. Perhaps, one of the most heart wrenching instance of loneliness, is the one of exclusion – to be consciously ostracized thru no fault of your own. It may be a situation where a person is afflicted with a medical or physical condition that is so abhorrent, or so emotionally exhausting, that most all friends *"don't want to get involved"*.

The loss of friends, when an individual has lost all hope, and is close to death's door, is often more demoralizing, and hurtful, than the original affliction.

A FRIEND IN NEED, IS A FRIEND INDEED!

MEMORIAL DAY

Memorial Day, formerly known as Decoration Day, is observed on the last Monday in May. It is a U.S. holiday in remembrance of members of the armed forces killed in war. Memorial Day, also known as Confederate Memorial Day, is observed on any of several days, in various southern states.

Although, Memorial Day observance was first officially proclaimed on May 5, 1868 by General John Logan, it was first observed on May 30th, 1868, when flowers were placed on the graves of Union and confederate soldiers at Arlington National cemetery.

Memorial Day was a balm, to heal the terrible wounds of division and hatred of recent past years of the Civil War, and to honor those who gave their all. The first state to officially recognize the holiday was New York in 1873; by 1890, it was recognized by all of the northern states. The South refused to acknowledge the day, honoring their dead on separate days, until after World War I. It was just a short time later, following WWI, when the holiday changed from honoring just those who died fighting in the Civil War, to honoring Americans fighting in any war.

Finally, congress passed the National Holiday Act of 1971, resulting in a three day weekend for Federal holidays. It is of note, that several southern states have additional separate days for honoring their dead.

As is often the case when good intentions are offered, the Holiday Act of 1971 is surrounded with controversy. It is the contention of many Americans that the Holiday Act, making Memorial Day a three day holiday, has severely diminished the importance, observance, and its true meaning. There is a movement to return to the original Memorial Day of observance (May 30th) because it is thought that the three day weekend has severely distracted from the spirit and the meaning of the day; To wit, on January 19, 1999 Senator Inouye and, on April19, 1999 Representative Gibbons introduced bills that would restore May 30th as the national observance day, for Memorial Day. The bills are still languishing in Congress.

It is true, that Memorial Day is an important time for us all to embrace, pause, honor and remember the sacrifice of those who gave their `last measure` for us. But, we all have, or will have, a loss of a loved one sooner or later that will cause terrible heartache and anguish. Even though the loss is a personal loss, the pain of that loss must be borne by each of us, in our own way, I see no reason why a National *Memorial Day* shouldn't include the memories of *all* lost loved ones, military or not; after all, loss of a loved one is painful, no matter the circumstances that caused the loss – *Just a thought.*

In 1915, inspired by the poem "In Flanders Fields," Moina Michaels wrote her own poem:

We cherish too, the poppy red

That grows on fields where valor led,

It seems to signal to the skies

That blood of heroes never dies.

She subsequently conceived of an idea to wear red poppies on Memorial Day. Her idea soon became associated with Memorial Day, not only in the United States, but also in many other countries. So, yes, there are "Poppy programs" that sell artificial poppies made by disabled veterans and, best of all, the poppy is a reminder for us all that many lives were lost, in honor, for their Nations welfare.

I don't know how you, the reader, feel when the subject "Memorial Day" is discussed, but it must be difficult for many, and certainly it is for me – for many reasons. It isn't just that so many, many lives were lost, but were lost before they had a chance to fulfill their destiny *and, were lost, needlessly.* Although, it is true that we all must follow the laws of nature, and will terminate our life's journey at some preordained time and place. It is one thing to die from an untreatable, incurable disease, but the disease (of War), that had afflicted the brave souls honored on Memorial Day, died from a malady that IS PREVENTABLE

WAR IS PREVENTABLE!

There is no treatment for the disease of War!

Common sense, honesty, understanding, love and goodwill

IS ---

THE ONLY VACCINE REQUIRED!

MEMORIES LOST

How is it possible to lose something that you physically never touched, or knew you had? How often have you heard "awe I forgot"? Or, "I wish I could remember what he said." Well, what we are alluding to is the capability of an amazing organ, the brain (mind), that has the ability to retain learned information and knowledge of past events and experiences, and to retrieve that information and knowledge; or, unfortunately, it may lose that capacity either on a temporary, or permanent basis, when afflicted with a disease such as an Alzheimer's affliction.

When discussing a topic such as memory loss, it may seem to be just another mishap that *just happens* to some unknown individual; we tend to shrug, or even pause and reflect for a moment, and then, continue on our way. But, what if that unhappy event happened to a loved one? What if that memory loss would change your lives forever, and would reduce a lifetime of happiness – to ashes?

Let me tell you a story about Alzheimer's disease,
and the horror of its consequences.

One day when I was attending to my wife's luncheon (of breaded fish) at the nursing home I, without thinking, asked her "Honey, do you remember that wonderful Canadian fish shore lunch that we had a few years ago?" She happily nodded that she remembered; but I knew she had no idea what I had just asked her, because she always nods her head in the affinitive – *to any question*; my wife is suffering from a strange malady (Alzheimer's disease), that is gradually destroying her brain, and robbing her of a lifetime of living memories. She is no longer able to remember any past remembrances – good, or bad. At that moment, I felt my world crumble, and I could almost not continue. I have no idea why I reacted so severely at that particular moment, because I was well aware that she had responded in a similar fashion, so many times before. I guess I was reminded, *once too often*, that our sixty- four years of married life, and all of our wonderful memories were -- memories lost!

Unexpectedly, I thought back to a time when I first met her, and knew that I had found the love of my life. I had become a helpless moth, drawn to the flame that offered me warmth, love and happiness. I knew then, that I would live, and die, within its warm embrace.

I remember, how I had tried to impress her by teaching her how to play golf (Never-mind that I was a novice golfer, myself); but, I think, it was the printed reindeer on my sweater that, upon chest muscle contractions, seemed to be running, that kept her spellbound (yes, there were chest muscles, when I was young).

Sadly, her relentless enemy (Alzheimer's disease) has ravaged her mind, and devastated her/our lives; but it cannot, and *will not, ever* be able to extinguish the deep embedded flame that, for so many years, had imparted such warmth, comfort, and love to me, and to all who knew her.

MEMORIES OF YEASTERYEARS

The human brain seems to do strange things, at times. How else can one explain the fact that now, at the age of 89 I am able to remember distant past experiences, but now, am unable to tell you what *transpired just a few hours ago.* Well, no matter, I will attempt to remember, and tell you, some of my experiences of yesteryear (the depression years of the late 20's and 30's.). I know that there have been many stories written about those brutal years, but I don't think there will be too many more accounts forthcoming (for obvious reasons).

It is well to remember, that the depression years affected a very large segment of our population. It wasn't unusual for a family to be forced out of their homes, because they were unable to pay the monthly rent. It is hard to believe, but a person could go to a bakery (0n certain days) and buy enough `day old` bread and cakes to fill two shopping bags – for a dollar. Yes, it was a time when the abnormal – was the norm.

The life of a `small kid` (ages 4-10) during the early 30's really wasn't all that bad. Oh sure, hunger was always a concern, but we found fun things to do, winter, or summer. Wintertime was always a fun time. We didn't build many igloos, but we sure did create formidable snow forts, for the frequent, fierce snowball fights. We would spend hours constructing the forts so that they would be sturdy, and be able to withstand frontal and rear attacks. We didn't have skis but, much to chagrin of our families, curtain rods worked pretty well on the icy sidewalks and streets.

Ah, yes, ice skating, in those days, was a popular sport for most of us future hockey `stars`. However, the ice skates were a real problem. Sure, there were `shoe` ice skates, but not for our insolvent crowd; we were content with the clamp on variety. The ice skate was simply a metal bar with one or two steel runners; it attached to our leather shoe sole by two clamps that could be tightened with a key. A leather or cloth belt around the ankle held the skate on the shoe – most of the time.

Hockey was our favorite skating sport, and was played wherever, and whenever we could find a patch of frozen water, frozen pond, or backyard `wet-area.` The two runner ice skate was the most sought after skate, because it enabled the player to walk, run, and to stop, or turn quickly; it even enabled the player to skate a little.

Our hockey games were awesome! A small can was our hockey puck, and the hockey sticks were, well, sticks. The scores were always sort of high, often in the 50 or 60 range, because, the goalies did everything in their power to get out of the path of a careening sharp, frozen can. The hockey games were usually halted, when the players were too frozen and bruised to continue – or, when it got too dark! Often, the games were sometimes ended prematurely, because the players had lost the leather soles of their shoes to the ice skate clamps.

It was during one of our games that I first heard the admonition "Watch out! You're going to get your eye put out, kid!"

I mentioned earlier that we didn't build too many igloos. Building an igloo was cold, hard work, but we did build a few; I suppose it was the challenge, and it did keep us busy. We packed snow into cardboard boxes, and then sprayed water on them; soon we had big ice blocks for our ice house. I have to admit, we surely were proud of our igloos. I'll bet some of my friends went on to become architects, or engineers because of those experiences garnered building "ice houses."

Then there was the making of the snowman. Ah, yes, the snow man. It seemed that a snowman appeared somewhere, every time there was the **right** kind of snow (heavy wet snowfall). It wouldn't do to have just any snowman; it had to be the biggest, best snowman around. The problem with a **big** snowman is that it requires **big** snowballs that have to be lifted one on another; that fact curtailed our enthusiasm somewhat.

I do have one memory that I will always cherish concerning the making of a snowman. When my granddaughters (twins) were five-years-old, their grandfather, with great flourish, volunteered to show them how to make a **good** snowman. Alas, by the time we commenced, the snow was sparse and difficult to work with.

The result was an anemic, skinny and, by all accounts, a pathetic specimen of a snowman. The worst thing that could have happened -- did! Someone took a picture of that poor excuse for a snowman! I am now reminded almost every winter, by my now adult granddaughters, of my **good** snowman that I had created for them. Ah, yes, such is life!! **What a wonderful memory!**

Lest you think that I spent all my youth playing and having fun, I will relate to you some of the other winter activities that I **do not** consider to be the good old days of winter.

I don't think there has ever been a word in the English language that makes me more upset and fighting mad than, "clinker"! Yes, clinker, as -- In furnace clinker.

You haven't lived unless you have encountered the fearsome, rock hard, foul-smelling, fused residue from the burning of bituminous coal. It was the "clinker" that prevented the ashes from dropping out of the furnace firebox. It took Herculean effort and the patience of Job to extricate this fused mass of coal impurities from the furnace's grates so that the fire could "breathe" again. If that wasn't bad enough, we then had to remove the ashes and relight the fire; it always went out during the night! All of this had to be done before going to school in the morning!! It was only later that we were able to obtain the much harder anthracite coal which had fewer impurities and didn't smell like sulfur. That fact made my life somewhat easier. I will *never* forget the "clinker"!!!!

Now that I think about it, the trials and tribulations of pushing a Model T Ford out of a snow bank and risking a fractured wrist when cranking to start it was a piece of cake compared to the dreaded "clinker problem"!!
At least, shoveling snow from sidewalks and driveways had its compensations (a nickel for a short one and a dime for a **long one).**

SUMMERTIME AND THE 'LIVIN' IS EASY

Sure, the winter time was great fun time for most of us during the 1930's, but we sure were cold most of the time. Ah, but summertime was the crème de la crème for most of us kids. Best of all, school was a bad memory, and, for three months, and there were FUN THINGS TO DO.

I was especially fond of playing marbles, and making and shooting "rubber guns". It took some skill to make a solid gun that would hold up under heavy use, and shooting knotted-up tire inner tube bands, for bullets. Special contests, each Saturday, were sponsored by the local playground to see who were the best marble 'shooters', and the best rubber gun marksman. The winner won the fantastic sum of five cents, and, GREAT FAME!

Of course, there was never a thought, or a possibility, to have a family summer, or winter vacation; but Thank goodness for the Salvation Army, they literally, saved my fragile 'growing up soul'.

Every summer, during the early 30's, our/ my Boy scout Troup #1 were fortunately, privileged, to spend two weeks at a 'wilderness' camp in southern Ohio. We, of course did our own cooking (most meals were loaded with pasta or potatoes). But, most importantly, the cost was reasonable – 5 dollars a week. The highlight of our camping trip was the visit by our parents at the end of the first week; who brought 'good stuff' (Pop, watermelon and chicken) for all their 'grown-up men.

I cannot say enough kind things about the Salvation Army's function during those desperate depression times. We, the have-nots, were treated with kindness, and respect. Their mentoring helped us grow straight, not gnarled and bent. Oh, did I mention the all-day movies were featured every Saturday in the Salvation Army auditorium – at a cost of -- 5 cents? It couldn't get any better than that; especially, since most of the movies were 'shootin' cowboys, and Indians!

As mentioned earlier, the summers and winters were not all playtime. ALL, the children were expected to help the family any way that they could. So, yes, we did shovel sidewalks, for a nickel, and driveways, for a dime. And, yes, we did have paper routes, and we did whatever we could to make a `buck`.

So, yes, those memories of yesteryears are bitter sweet. Although things were abnormal during depressions years, of the late 20's and 30's, somehow, or other, we managed quite well because we were ALL in the same boat – the abnormal – WAS the normal. When it was all said and done, we learned that:

When the going gets tough, the tough get going

There is no free lunch; you have to work for it

It's a good feeling to succeed in something

Kindness, is contagious

Amen!

MOURNING DOVES

I heard the call of an angel this morning!

I, unexpectedly, heard the repeated soft mournful calls of a mourning dove, and it shocked me! It was a fairly warm morning, while visiting my angel (wife) at her sanctuary (nursing home); when over and above the omnipresent sounds of the traffic, and commerce chatter, we heard mournful calls `wooo, woo, woo` ("where are you -- where are you, where are you.)" I am well aware that my interpretation of the dove's calls may be incorrect, but her `tone of voice` sure did sound familiar to me (soft, but authoritative); I had heard that compelling call so many times in the past from my own, now wounded, angel.

As we sat outside, waiting for lunch to be served at the nursing home, I looked at my wife and thought to myself, how wonderful it would be if, she too, would again be capable of calling softly "where are you, where are you". But, alas, she is no longer able to call to me, or tragically, even remember who I am -- Alzheimer's disease has rendered her mind incapable of thought and memory. It was a blessing to hear the bird's soft calls, and to witness the delight on my wife's face as she sat in her wheelchair, mesmerized by the soothing song of an `angel` calling to her.

That evening, following the gentle doves musical rendition, I had the feeling that I really should know a little more about one of nature's magnificent creatures, the dove; after all, shouldn't an eighty-eight year old person know an Angel whom he might meet, anon -- and thank her for a splendid performance that uplifted, and brightened our spirits?

And, now, THE MOURNING DOVE

I suppose I shouldn't admit this, but early on, in my life, I always knew the soft, melodic `wooo-woo-woo song that I heard in the distance was a *MORNING dove;* it was only much later, that I realized that it was a MOURNING dove. Well, no matter, at least I knew it was a dove; and, after all, I usually did hear their melodic songs *in the morning*.

There are several other doves that differ slightly from the mourning dove, but other than coloring, are essentially the same species. The mourning dove is the most abundant bird on the continent; and, unfortunately, the most hunted and killed, each year. It is stated that well over 20 million birds are shot each year. It is estimated that there are about 120 million (doves) birds on the continent, but are not on the critical survivors list at this time. It should be noted that the mourning doves close relative, the Passenger Pigeon, was not as fortunate, and is now extinct -- they were shot to extinction, by `brave hunters`.

For the uninitiated, the mourning dove is another one of nature's exquisite creations of form and function. This tiny graceful, slender tailed, small headed athlete (measuring 11-12inches, and weighing 4.5 -6 oz.), is one of nature's fastest flying birds (speeds of 45 -55 mi mph). Hopefully, their speed and dexterity will allow these messengers of song and beauty to outmaneuver, and survive the brave, witless, hunter's killing fields.

God speed dear friends,

Sing, my Angels --- Sing!

PS,

It is abundantly clear that our Angels, the doves, are guardians of all God's children. One needs to look no further than the bosom of a lovely Sand dollar, lying on the bottom of the seas, to affirm their presence; because, there, within their lovely shells, lays 5 beautiful white doves, awaiting the calls of love.

MY BROTHER'S KEEPER

We, all, are brothers and sisters. We, all, are vulnerable to the unpredictable challenges that life presents to us. There is no one on this earth who is immune from unexpected disasters or illness; we are merely short term, travelers on the journey of life. Shakespeare's Macbeth's views of life:

o-morrow

and to-morrow, and

to-morrow,

Creeps in this petty pace from day to day
To the last syllable of recorded time,
And all our yesterdays have lighted fools
The way to dusty death. Out, out brief candle!
Life's but a walking shadows, a poor player,
That struts and frets his hour upon the stage,
And then is heard no more; it is a tale
Told by an idiot, full of sound and fury,
Signifying nothing.

Yes, we are, whether we like it or not, vulnerable to the whims of nature, and life's capricious malevolent secrets of life -- we are not immune! So, what are we to do? Would it be prudent to procure life insurance? Yes, of course, but would that protect you from the *desolation, and loss of life's goodness that only a brother, or sister can offer? No, it is abundantly clear, that the `goodness of life` is only possible when there is the* support and kindness of a `close` human being.

It is true that `care giving` is a virtue offered by the majority of the world's cultures; but vary, of course, not because of the lack of resolve, but unavailability of resources. So, what are we to do? Hopefully, the answer is, a sincere pledge that "We will do the best that we can".

Several months ago, I had written a short story titled "Where have they all gone?" It was **my** 'cry in the wilderness'; when, after months and months of my daily visits to the nursing home to care for my wife who is afflicted with Alzheimer's disease, I was distressed to realize that all of her "friends", and even some of her family members, could not find the time for a brief visit to acknowledge that she was still alive, and needed reassurance and kindness. It seems that the aphorism -- there, but for the grace of God, go I" had been forgotten. Unfortunately, what goes around -- comes around; and alas, there will inevitably be heard, once again in the future, beseeching cries from many others, out in the 'wilderness'.

There are no treasures in this world that could possibly compare in value, or importance, to the gift of 'life', and the love and caring of our fellow man. How awful would it be if a person had a thousand pounds of gold, but could not buy an ounce of love and caring with it; but yet, would be happy for a lifetime, if when penny-less, was blessed with the love of brotherhood.

So, yes, we must all be our Brother's keepers. I will close with the final few paragraphs of a short story I had recently written, titled, 'Home is where the heart is'. It is a bitter-sweet story of the finality of one's life journey, and the true meaning -- of love and brotherhood.

HOME IS WHERE THE HEART IS

"It would appear, that The Supreme Curator of all creatures large and small, had planned our life's final journey meticulously well; because, with the passing of time (year, after, year) of my presence, and being with her for lunch and supper on a daily basis, has helped her accept her fate, even as her Alzheimer's disease was slowly draining her body's treasures and mind.

And so, for the past many years (5 years at home, and 4 years in the nursing home), my love and caring for her has been physically, and mentally difficult, but wonderfully heartwarming for me. I know that there are many medical journal warnings, and sad reports concerning stress related outcomes for caregivers, but I honestly believe, that her need for my love, help and understanding, has for the past 9 years, kept me functional, and physically active, as I rapidly approach my 89th birthday.

YES,

WE ALL, ARE, OUR BROTHER'S KEEPERS

OLT TOO SOON SCHMART TOO LATE

It seems that I've heard the aphorism (adage) about age and wisdom, forever. I really never knew exactly what it meant. Oh, I knew what getting old meant, but the part about getting smart sort of escaped me. It kind of worries me because I never `felt` schmart when I was very young, and I certainly don't feel `schmart` now. Well, maybe I'm just a slow learner, and since I have a `way-to-go` (I'm only 89 years old), maybe I'll still have time to `schmarten` up.

I know that the proverb `olt too soon, schmart to late` is said, to be said, by the Dutch, but I think most of us, of the thinking population of the world, have also thought, or said, the same words many, many times in our lives. The problem with being smart is: **if you're smart, you will know HOW dumb you are!** The problem with being dumb is: **if you DON'T know that you're dumb, you alas, will think you're smart**. Such was the case for me before I got to be `olt too soon`, and schmart too late -- let me explain. Although there are many exceptions, it is generally thought that the years between 20 and 40, are our "honey years". It is a period of time when we do our best; it is a time when our `juices` are flowing mightily, and our desires and needs for recognition, accomplishment, and yes, for love, are overflowing.

I suppose you could say that I was smart early on, because I realized that I wasn't very smart, and I realized that if I didn't get some `schmarts` I would have a difficult time in life. So -- I decided to go back to school -- to get my `schmarts` when I was in my `middle` twenties; I decided I would "go all the way" and become a doctor.

For the first few years of `gathering schmarts` I continued to `feel dumb`, but amazingly felt an inner satisfaction, and knew, that whatever was in store for me, I would endure and succeed. And so it was that after 12 years of struggle, I had finally `gathered some schmarts` -- and was now a physician; I thought I was the best Doc in the world! THE OLD DUTCH

APHORISM WAS WRONG; I was YOUNG, AND, SCHMART! Ah yes? But, Could I have been wrong -- very wrong? Perhaps!

The initial years of medical practice were difficult, but exhilarating for me because everything was now a new life experience. There were many problems encountered that required great diligence, and were worrisome, but when the outcome turned out to be a happy one, there was great euphoria; and alas, there was great depression when sad outcomes were encountered.

As the years swiftly passed, it became obvious that things were not the way they should be for me... So, by the 15th year of medical practice, I had gradually begun to feel more inadequate, even though my practice was very successful. I felt that I should do more, even though I had tried desperately to keep current in medical knowledge. By the time I had been in medical practice for 25 years, I continued to feel inadequate, but gradually began to realize that there will always be more to learn and know than I was capable of mastering -- but I continued to do the best that I could.

Finally, after 30 plus years of medical practice, I had reached a compromise with my demanding `Medical knowledge Demon` that had, for so long, tempted, and sorely challenged me throughout my Medical life; I finally realized that I, at the age of 89, could never know all there is to know about medicine, or the vagaries of life. And, yes, I finally realized that the best I could do in my medical and personal life **would have to be good enough**, and thus, was comforted; an acceptable compromise had been reached.

The aphorism --

OLT TOO SOON SCHMART TOO LATE

IS, SO VERY, VERY TRUE!

Lofdoc (Lots of Fishing Doc)

PS,

Without ambition one starts nothing

Without work one finishes nothing.

The prize will not be sent to you.

You have to earn it.

Ralph Waldo Emerson

Dare to be what you are

And learn to resign

With a good grace all

That you are not, and to

Believe in your own individuality

Henri-Frederic Amiel

"OUT OF THE BLUE"

It's a small world, Charlie Brown! It seems, sometimes, that someone is watching over us, and suddenly, *"out of the blue"*, presents us with a present of great value – the gift of a lost friend, or a long absent family member.

I can't tell you how many times I have heard, or read, of a friend finding a "lost" dear friend, who had suddenly appeared, out of the blue, on a street corner; or when a telephone call is answered and a voice asks "Are you --- from ---? Well, lo and behold, now that I am far advanced into my senior years (87) I was blessed with two such "out of the blue" miracles, when I answered the telephone and heard "Are you -- who --?" As you must know, the thrill of hearing the voice asking "are you – ", and then after you hesitatingly say yes, realize that you are hearing the "voice of happiness of the distant past" (70 years ago); well, even an old-man is capable of shedding a tear of happiness!

A few years ago, I received a telephone call from California. The person asked if my name was "Andy". I, of course, became very defensive, because I didn't recognize the young female voice, and I didn't know any person living in California. My fears were quickly dispelled when she explained that she was Susie, the daughter of my long lost dear friend named Louie T. She said: Maybe you would better remember him if I mentioned his "old time name" that you and he often used in fun. She quickly asked, do you remember "Luigi"? I, of course, remembered Louie, how could I ever forget him –he was the best friend that I have ever had. She then said "please hold the line for a moment." It was at that moment that I realized that my old friend was still alive, and I was about to hear, and speak, to the "gentle ghost" that had been lost --- for so many years.

When I heard a voice say "Hello", I was unable to speak; I choked and had a difficult time controlling my emotions – and tears. Shortly thereafter, his daughter said, please wait a few moments, my Dad is having a little trouble with his voice.

We eventually were able to briefly update recent events in our lives, and even reminisce a little about the "good old days". Our initial talk was followed by many letters, pictures etc. Approximately one year later, I received a telephone call from Susie to inform me that my friend Louie had passed -- over -- into the great beyond. She wanted me to know that her father was so happy that he had had the opportunity to find you again – and, to say, "Goodbye, dear friend."

PS,

Louie "Luigi" and I were very close friends throughout our early school years during the 1930's and early 1940's. Luigi was a friend who would always do what he could to help you, if he could; he was a gentle and kind human being. Although he always, laughingly, would say "look at my big schnoz (nose), I'll never get a girl- friend"; actually, he was quite handsome, in a rugged sort of way. I'm sure his wife of many years, and his daughter, Susie, would agree with my assessment. But, that was vintage Louie, a modest and lovable guy.

World War II did manage to separate us. I had enlisted in the Navy, and Louie, into the Army. It would be a separation that would last until the day I received that phone call from a lovely voice from California; from Susie, Louie's daughter. *I had waited almost seventy years for that phone call!*

It is a strange thing, but throughout those many years, I would, for no apparent reason think about him, and wonder what had happened to him. When I began writing short stories "in my later, senile years" I wrote the short story "Friends and Friendships"; it was written with Louie in mind. Yes, **True Friends do come in, when all others have gone out.**

Now, I Know, that that aphorism is so very true.

Rest in peace, my dear friend

Lastly, those individuals are truly fortunate who have at least one good friend, and they are doubly blessed, *if that friend is their chosen life's partner.*

My second epiphany (an experience of sudden and striking realization) occurred in more recent times; proving that serendipity (luck) often plays an important role in our lives.

Believe it or not, the tuning of a piano, in a nearby city, resulted in my finding a close relative who had been "lost" for near 70 years. Yes, the relative was "lost", but unbeknownst to me, lived just a few short miles away. Even more remarkable, it was *my son* who was indirectly the catalyst that made it possible for me to find my last living cousin (1st cousin). Let me explain.

My son, who *repairs* and tunes pianos, recently was contracted to tune an individual's piano in a nearby suburb. Remarkably, the man who had his piano tuned just happened to be Jim (my last remaining, eighty year-old first cousin). As luck would have it, Jim was not home at the time when the piano was tuned. Later, Jim needed to have the piano tuned once again, and after a long search his wife, Sally, finally found the invoice with the piano tuners name and address in a place she had previously placed it (so she could easily find it the next time)! This time, when looking at the previous invoice, his wife asked Jim "isn't this piano tuners name the same as that of your cousin, you know, the cousin you have mentioned so many times before? Yes, of course, it was.

When the day for the piano tuning arrived, Jim made it a point to be present when the piano was to be tuned. His first question of the tuner was "Is your father's name, Andy, and, did he live in -----? Yes, of course. Jim then startled my son, the piano tuner, when he said "Your father is my first cousin!" And, then, he followed that revelation, with "Do you want to see a picture of your Great Grandfather? And, so, after so many years ------!

Now, the rest of the story!

I guess, it isn't too unusual for families and relatives to occasionally separate and pursue different directions in life, but finding Jim and his lovely wife, Sally, has meant a great deal to me.

My mother and Jim's mother were sisters. Tragically, my mother died one year after my birth, in 1928; my father, with four children, never remarried. The following years of the severe depression of the late 20's & early 30's, and subsequent poverty, resulted in displacement of many families, and so it was with my family.

I must admit, that over the years, I had often thought about the whereabouts and fate of my relatives – now I gratefully know!

Perseverance

If you were asked: "What human attribute, or quality, do you consider to be most important for achieving success" -- how would you respond; would your answer be -- Perseverance?? That question is not just a haphazard silly quiz to see if you are `paying attention`, it is a very huge package of human involvement encased in a very small, but ubiquitous human emotion (passion), called -- **desire -- a desire** `to achieve a goal`. Of course, a desire is laudable, and I suppose, we all have had a few `desires` in our lifetime, but, did we always get what we desired when the going got tough, and achieving our goal would require perseverance if we were to be successful? But, let's be honest; unless 'that desire' was truly important to achieve, we would somehow manage to continue without fulfilment -- thinking -- it just isn't worth the trouble to persevere.

But hold on, I would like to make a confession at this time.

As I thought, and mulled over the topic --Perseverance, I, LOFDOC, your author, realized that the subject, PERSEVERANCE, was more than just a `topic subject` for me; it **was truly "a way of life," for me -- it was the only way I could possibly have existed on** this Planet; I **Had** to be determined, and perseverant, or all would have been lost.

I will continue.

A MINI AUTOBIOGRAPHY

Ah, but what if you didn't know, or realize, that you were afflicted with a `bone-aching` desire? What if you just thought that `it would be good` to be a doctor, or, a cowboy, or, or an ---? What if you, without knowing why -- you suddenly decided to be a doctor; but what then? Well, I guess it all depends on why I was ` doctor--desire- afflicted ` in the first place. Ah, now we have come to the reason why we are here; how would a young lad, afflicted with a desire to be a doctor, know why it was that he wanted to become a doctor? The answer is in the Stars and the mind -- *perhaps there was a deep-seated reason.*

Let's attend to the affliction (the need to be a physician) source first, because how `deep` is the desire impact on the psyche, will oft'time determine life's direction and future happiness.

Is it possible, that the events which occurred shortly after I was born cause such a deep, searing, mental scar that would affect my future direction in life? If so, yes, having lost my mother because hospitalization and medical care were refused her because there were no funds to pay for, and treat her diseased gallbladder. Would there not be deep resentment and anger? It is true, my distrust of the medical profession became so severe, that I, for many years refused to enter, or even be near a hospital; such was my deep frustration and pain.

It seemed that God had deserted me early on in my life. Soon after my mother's death, I was placed in an extended home with a relative, when I developed an obstruction to my trachea (wind-pipe), and required emergency surgery (tracheotomy) to save my life. Things did not improve for me, or my family, because soon thereafter, the Nation, and my family became mired in the great depression of the late, 1920's and early, 1930's. It is of note that other than my early encounter with the medical profession, I, nor any member of my family ever had, or wanted to have, contact with the medical profession during those heartbreaking, poverty-torn years.

The following few years were stressful, and poverty laden, and were not conducive for learning, or development of social skills -- it was for me, a time of struggle to survive; although, somehow, I did manage to barely graduate from high school.

It was in 1944, and World War II had inflamed the world, and changed the lives of millions of young men. *It was the events of the next two years that formulated, and determined my future course in life.*

Many times in life, events and `happenings, ` just seem to -- well, happen. It was during the fearful time of WWII in 1944, that I, young lad, of 17, decided to enlist in the Navy -- to be a submariner. However, the Navy decided that our fighting forces were in need of medical personnel so, I, along with many others, was assigned to be a medical corpsman. Being assigned to be a medical corpsman was like a death sentence for me; it was the last profession on this earth that I would have ever wanted. But, I had no choice in the matter, so I decided that I would do the best that I could; but going back to school was difficult for me. **It was then, at that time, that I truly experienced an epiphany**; I began to realize that I wasn't stupid, and that I was capable of learning, if I *persevered*; and yes, even if it was to learn about medical subjects. Following Naval Medical Corp School, I was assigned, eventually, to a small clinic at a naval aircraft carrier service base at Brunswick, Maine. It was there that I felt needed and fulfilled, and yes, it was then that I vowed -- "God willing, I will become a doctor."

Following the successful conclusion of the war, the nation slowly returned to normalcy; but, it was the beginning of a long, difficult, fearsome journey for me. I really wasn't prepared to navigate the difficult crossroads and hurls encountered on my medical odyssey to becoming a physician, but I was deeply committed --- nothing short of death could abort my journey; I vowed to succeed. I would, with perseverance, be the best darn Doctor around, and swore, that as sure as there are stars in the heavens, no person will ever be neglected, or refused medical care for lack of funds -- that was my silent, solemn commitment. I fulfilled my vow, during thirty plus years of solo Medical Practice.

So, dear reader, you now have read the confession, and abbreviated Autobiography of your Author, LOFDOC. It was written, not for praise or applause, but to remind us all that success is not a gift freely given; it is often presented to the recipient with a costly price tag that need be paid with sweat, toil and commitment, and at times, can only be accomplished, with sacrifice and --- Perseverance.

PH,

The *paragraphs* appearing below were taken from a book, LOFDOC'S STORYS SHORT AND SWEET, written by LOFDOC, a few years ago. The story:

`The practice of medicine and its best kept secrets` ---

"I acknowledge the fact that the medical community, in by-gone days, did not always respond to the needs of the sick and injured, without first demanding financial compensation. I am a first-hand witness to the medical community's *sometimes* heartless disregard for life. My own mother died in 1928, at the age of twenty-seven; she was refused hospitalization because payment could not be guaranteed. Today, that tragedy would never happen, and a young mother of four small children would not die because she could not pay for medical attention to a gangrenous gallbladder.

Today, even though the present day physician is buffeted from many directions, there has been one constant commitment – we will never refuse our services to the ill or injured, regardless of the patient's ability to pay for those services. To my knowledge, no person in need of medical care has ever been turned away for lack of funds. A large majority of non-profit and many for-profit hospitals provide medical care via their emergency rooms. They may, and do sustain losses of millions of dollars because of non-payment; but, they would *never* refuse proper care to all in need."

QUACKERY

Although the title, quackery, may sound lighthearted (free from care, or seriousness), it is, what it is; it is fraud, dishonesty, deception, trickery, flimflam – and worse. Of course, quackery probably has existed since mankind first meandered around the surface of our planet, so why discuss it now? Well, I guess, it is like most things in life, we, who are still able to think, and are personally involved in some way with gross deception, feel the need for ventilation -- or we will burst! Quackery can be found in almost all facets of human relationships; but quackery that involves the health and lives of innocent, trusting souls is not only dangerous, it is tantamount to grand larceny, and even murder in some cases.

Over the many years (60) that I have been privileged to be a Medical Physician (Internal Medicine) in the state of Ohio I, unfortunately, have observed many instances of quackery of one type or another that had caused various degrees of suffering, disability, financial loss, and in some cases even death. It is comforting to know that most all the quackery occurrences were legally and/ or decisively thwarted, or prevented.

Since the definition of quackery infers dishonesty, trickery and deception, one need only look around, to easily see examples of fraud (advertisements in newspapers, radio, and not least, the computer. A large number of quackery instances that afflict us are not actually seen as being fraud or greed, but rather, are seen as "aggressive promotion" e.g. "front men" telling us that certain food additives are bad for us, and that we should switch to their "organic", or "natural" products. And, of course, who hasn't seen misleading advertisements of dietary supplements, vitamins, herbs, and non-prescriptive drugs? This latter group of "falseness" is a classic example of -- corporate and advertising deception (quackery).

Another instance of quackery, that isn't *necessarily* quackery, can often be seen in medical research and scientific research. For example, several years ago, in a leading medical hospital, patients were subjected to "medical" procedures that can only be considered quackery. The Doctors, who were involved, were searching to find a treatment for coronary heart disease (CAD). The first attempt involved making a simple incision in the chest (over the sternum), and then quickly closing the wound without further surgery. I am at a loss as to what they expected to accomplish; perhaps to show that sometimes "mind over matter" is the cause of the chest pain? The second procedural attempt to treat (CAD) was to actually open the chest and pericardium (heart sac), and insert talcum powder. It was thought that talcum powder would cause inflammation, which in turn would create an ideal milieu for new blood vessels to form; and thus, create vascular bridges across the clogged coronary arteries. These two procedures were classic quackery since there wasn't a proven scientific basis ; yet, in view of the fact that they were performed by ethical Physicians, and were not done in malice, or for gain, they would not ever be termed quackery – but, it WAS quackery non the less!. Of note, however, later research (in the same hospital), led to the wonderful diagnostic procedure of `heart catheterization` which enables us to actually see the heart's entire vascular tree. Heart catheterization has saved million upon millions of individuals who would otherwise have died from heart disease. Hooray, for quackery (at times) – and, for serendipity ("fortunate happenstance").

And, now, I will tell you of two actual instances of `honest to goodness` quackery that I had personally encountered.

Several years ago, while I was still in medical practice, and was, at the time, president of the hospital medical staff, two physicians (a husband and wife partnership), were involved in a scheme of unprecedented callousness. The husband was a surgeon, and the wife was a Gynecologist. Although they were skilled in their chosen fields, their ethics were, at best, suspect. It was only after numerous complaints from patients, and subsequent fact-finding by authorities, that it was possible to expose, and terminate their quackery. It seems that the couple referred patients to one another for surgery, whether it was medically necessary, or not. It was only after the hospital pathologists had sounded the alarm that many of their surgical specimens submitted for analysis during surgery were found to be normal tissue, and were free of disease, that their nefarious money- making quackery was ended, and their medical licenses' revoked.

And finally, it is a recently encountered instance of blatant quackery that compelled me to write this article.

Believe it or not, my story begins with a birthday card.

Several weeks ago, I mailed a birthday card to a dear friend who lives in Florida. My old friend had suffered a severe back injury several years ago, that in spite of multiple surgeries and rehabilitation efforts, had left him with permanent loss of almost all the muscles and nerves of both legs. He now has great difficulty walking without considerable assistance.

I tell you these facts, not for sympathy, but to explain the sordid circumstances that he recently endured at the hands of a "medical" professional. After my friend had received my birthday card, he called me long distance to thank me for remembering him on his birthday. It was during that telephone conversation that he told me he had answered a newspaper "flyer" that touted a treatment that would grow new nerves and muscles, by injecting the legs with a miracle drug. When my friend read the article, he was ecstatic; there now was hope that he would be medically whole again, and would be free of pain. As you might imagine, I was horrified and saddened when he told me that, because I knew his injuries were such that there was no hope of ever growing new nerves or muscles, or repairing his destroyed spinal cord. Our further conversation revealed that he had paid a large sum of money, and was scheduled to receive bi-weekly painful injections into his legs, for many weeks. I was relieved to learn that, at least, his "doctor of miracles" *was not a medical doctor.*

I asked him to please inform his regular physician (an internal medicine MD) about what he was doing. I knew the reaction and response he would get.

A few days later, my friend called to tell me that his regular physician was greatly disturbed that *anyone* would so degrade the medical profession, that he gave him a letter to give to his "doctor" of miracles, demanding that all treatments be immediately stopped, and to be recompensed for all funds paid.

Since this story is an ongoing true saga, I have no idea what the outcome concerning the funds will be – stay tuned. Perhaps, and hopefully, the medical community will work to see justice served, and put this heartless, dishonest bugger, where he belongs.

So, alas!

It seems that quackery is still very much alive, and kicking!

PS,

Apparently, the letter from my friend's doctor did some good. I recently learned that the charlatan did refund all the monies except for the two "treatments" provided earlier, and plans to contact the BBB, and the State Medical Board. Perhaps, soon, another Quack will receive his just rewards!

REINCARNATION OF A SINGER

Several years ago, I had the good fortune to know a young man, Eric Hinderbland, who lived, and breathed music; he was born to sing. 'Brian Crower' once wrote, "God breathes lyrics out of us." Yes, he was a young man who wanted nothing more in life than to sing -- yes, to sing. His life was consumed with 'the sound of music'; he wanted desperately to be an operatic singer. His voice, according to his many admirers 'was as pure and captivating as an Angel's Sigh, and as robust as the Devil's Cry;' but yes, his voice was the 'sound of heaven' on this Earth!'

"THE SONG," is a story that chronicles young Eric Hinderbland life; a life of hope and promise, and heartbreaking turn of events, but then ---- miraculously, ------; but hold on, let me recount the bitter-sweet story of Eric Hinderbland with a story titled, 'The Song', before I breathlessly, tell you --- the rest of the story.

Happiness and prosperity continued for Oscar and Anna Hinderbland. By 1928 there were four children (Eric, born in 1927), and were all thought to be musically inclined, but it was Oscar and Anna's hope that, Eric, would someday become a fine singer.

Although the depression was severe during the 30's, and the Hinderbland family did suffer financially, but they managed to find five dollars a week for Eric's voice lessons. There was little doubt in their minds that Eric would be a world-class tenor in the years to come.

Eric's life was filled with music. He especially loved classical music and sang whenever and wherever he had an opportunity. He sang in many choirs during his grade school and high school years. When an opera performed in his hometown of Toledo, Ohio, he was often seen trying to sneak into the auditorium to hear and see the performers. It wasn't unusual to hear him sing early in the morning while preparing to go to school and then hear him sing on his way home from school in the afternoon. People soon began to prepare their activities so that they could be present to hear his magnificent renditions. There was no doubt in anyone's mind that they were listening to greatness. Oscar and Anna were convinced that they had given the world a truly great gift – they were ecstatic!

The time came for a fateful decision to be made that would affect Eric's life. The family decided that since he was soon to graduate from high school, Eric should be evaluated by a prestigious music professor to plan for his future training and direction. It was this decision that spelled disaster for Eric and his family.

After the initial consultation with the professor, Eric smiled and asked him "Do you think I will be a great singer as my parents and many others believe"? Much to his horror and disbelief, he heard "No, I do not think you will *ever* be great".

To this day, Eric has no recollection of how he got home that day. He did remember asking the professor to please not tell his parents of his determination. He then told his parents and friends that he was on schedule, but that it was going to be a hard road to pursue.

Several days later, another disaster befell Eric. He awakened one morning to find that he could not talk above a whisper – he had lost his voice. After several physicians had examined him and after many days had passed, it was determined that his malady was permanent and that his singing career was at an end.

Needless to say, his parents and friends were terribly distressed. They bravely told him that there are other things in life besides singing and that music could still be an integral part of his life.

Strangely enough, Eric didn't really feel too badly about losing his voice. He did miss singing but developed the attitude of "Well, win some, lose some – you can't win them all"!

Finally, his high school graduation day arrived. All the graduating seniors were on the stage and the ceremony commenced. As was the custom, the **Lord's Prayer,** or an appropriate offering was to be sung by the next best vocalist in the school choir (Eric was the best vocalist of the school until his recent illness). Then as his surrogate approached the microphone, center stage, he suddenly became unsteady on his feet, began to sweat and then collapsed – he fainted! Confusion followed; what was to be done?

Suddenly, from the back row of the congregated students on the stage, a beautiful sound was heard over the din and confusion. **Ave Maria** was heard. At first tenuous and soft, then firm and full, it was Eric's beautiful voice saying in heavenly tones, **Ave Maria**.

An amazing transition overtook the auditorium as he continued to sing. Total silence ensued. No one dared to sneeze or cough, heads were bowed, and some were seen to make the cross. It was the most beautiful song that was ever heard at a commencement, or anywhere else.

After the final notes were sung, the audience remained motionless and silent for several minutes. There was no need to applaud perfection, they had heard -- **THE SONG.**

Epilogue

Eric had "lost" and then "found" his voice. How could that happen? Let me explain by way of an example. We all know that electric transmission lines have a fuse or a circuit breaker to prevent overloading the line which, if not short-circuited, would cause a fire or worse. Well, it appears that the human brain also has safeguards known as the subconscious mind that acts as a fuse or circuit breaker in times of severe peril or possible destruction of the conscious mind. In Eric's case, he was told that he would never be a great singer. This was the most terrible scenario that could have befallen him. He was in danger of losing his sanity or worse. If, then, he lost his voice, how could **he** be responsible for being a failure – after all, it wasn't his fault! *His mental health was preserved!*

He "found" his voice because he had always dreamed of singing AVE MARIA at his own graduation. His need to do so was the compelling force that enabled him to, once again, "find" his voice.

And now, the rest of the story

The following days and months following Eric's High School graduation, were the happiest days of Eric Hinderbland life; he had miraculously 'found' his voice, when he, 'and all the World' thought it was lost. Although he was elated that many compliments kept pouring in from folks who had heard him sing the "Song," he, 'down deep,' was confused, and worried that he might 'lose' his voice again; he did think that "If it happens again (lose his voice) I will go crazy".

But as time passed, and his voice became stronger, he convinced himself that having lost his voice was just 'one of those things that happen,' he would now work harder to be the best vocalist he could be; maybe, just maybe, that Professor who told him that he would never be a great singer -- could be wrong.

And, so, he realized, that as all great achievers of the world realize, talent is not always enough for success; hard work, perseverance, intelligence, and sweat are required, and (yes, of course), serendipity (luck) is always welcome. Young Eric -- was committed, and vowed, -- "I **will** be a great Operatic singer someday"!

The next few years were challenging, painful years. Eric experienced periods of joy, and deep dejection, but he never faltered. He gradually gained the respect of the 'music' community, and subsequently gained more and more important roles in various operas in Italy and beyond. *It would be only a matter of time until he will reach the pinnacle of the mountain, of stardom; that elusive mountain, that mountain of hope that he had been climbing for oh, so long.*

Destiny once again befriends Eric

It is no secret that baseball players often spend their day-off, watching a baseball game; and it so it for musicians with music. There was one opera that Eric treasured above all others; it is Mozart's "The Marriage of Figaro

(Le nozze di Figaro). Although Eric studied and practiced the lead 'tenor role' for many operas (to be prepared -- just in case he was needed), he especially loved Mozart's opera Figaro's Basilio. As luck would have it, a well-known traveling opera company was to feature a one night stand of 'The Marriage of Figaro 'in the small town where he was visiting a friend; needless to say, Eric HAD to attend their performance.

It was during the First Act of the Marriage of Figaro, that suddenly, the tenor Basilio, the slimy music teacher, collapsed on the stage. Of course, confusion followed; what was to be done? It was at that point, that Eric's friend got up and went back stage. Soon thereafter, the management came out and whispered to Eric "Can you be Basilio?" Eric, without hesitation said "Yes, yes, I will be 'Basilio.'"

It was that night's magnificent performance of Basilio that was the serendipitous turning point in Eric's Music world. Soon thereafter, he was inundated with major operatic roles.

Eric's Graduation day; The Song Ave Maria,

And Destiny ---

Conquered his Mountain

RELUCTANTLY, HE HANDED OVER THE KEY

There are many words heard in our daily lives that convey emotion, fraternity, love, hate, etc., but, the words "reluctantly, he handed over the key" carry a heavy burden of implied sadness, and distress. Probably, the most hated words in the English language are the words "hand over your car keys," when spoken to an **old man, or woman**, who, after several car accidents, are required to 'give up' their last vestige of independence and freedom -- the keys to their car; so, yes, they sadly, with tears, -- **reluctantly, handed over the key**, and lost their cherished 'chariot of freedom' -- and thus, *Their* -- freedom.

I suppose, many of us "not so old" folks, will probably have to 'reluctantly,' hand over the key, at some point in our lives, of assets that had made our lives livable. Imagine the horror of having to 'hand over the key to your bank account, or the key to your home' -- a home that you have lived in for a lifetime.

Ah, yes, just when one appears to be immersed in sorrow after hearing the many accounts having the words "Reluctantly, he handed over the key", a burning light of happiness and fraternity may suddenly materialize, and restore your faith in humanity; **after,** you have read **my story,** titled: "Reluctantly, he handed over the key".

Allow me to tell you a story of compassion, and brotherhood that will make you proud to be a member of the Human Race,

Many years ago, there lived an individual who lived, and worked, in a small southern village; and who, for many, was truly, a blessed angel. Oh, he wasn't the 'religious' kind of angel; he was 'Old Doc' Adams who seemed to always to 'be there' for you when medical help was needed. It was said of him, "Whenever you get sick, or need advice, our Angel, Doc. Adams, will always be there for you."

'Old Doc.', as he was lovingly called, lived a humble life. He had lost his wife early-on in their marriage from a medical mishap during the birth of his son. Although he was always referred to as 'old Doc, he was still a young man in his late twenties -- *he just looked old* (some attributed his aged appearance to excessive stress).

As the years swiftly passed, and stress continued, poor old Doc Adams began to slow down, and was heard to say "I'm just a little tired; but, I'll be OK, tomorrow". But, his 'tomorrow,' never came; 'old' Doc died, before his 50th birthday.

When his son Tomaso was finally contacted, and notified of his father's death he, heartbroken, arrived at the village only to learn that his father's estate was bankrupt, and there was a sizable debt attachment. But how could that be? Doc had a huge practice; but, it was well known by the villagers that 'old doc' rarely asked for payment for his services, and they, for their shame, never insisted on paying him.

And so, it was decided to auction off all of Doc's possessions, so that closure of his estate could be possible.

Incredibly, Doc had few possessions that were considered worthy enough to hold an auction. Oh, he did have an old 'beat-up' jeep, and a well-worn "doctor-bag", but that was it. He did not leave a will, but had said, early-on, that he would give all his earthly possessions to the people of the village. But, at the insistence of his son, Tomaso, an auction was held.

It was thought that the auction would take only a few minutes because there were only a few household furnishings, a power mower, and some tools -- and -- his old jeep 'that he drove for years' and, of course, his precious old Doctor bag that the villagers, knew and loved so well.

Very quickly, most all the articles were sold for a pittance, and the only articles remaining to be auctioned, were the old jeep, and the 'doctor bag'.

The bidding opened for the jeep and bag was a low bid of $100 dollars. Following the opening bid, there was a long silence, when a bid for $5000 dollars was heard. Then, quickly, the auction seemed to have a life of its own. The following bidding then escalated into a frenzy of financial numbers, and finally, ended with the final bid of $60,000 dollars.

The bidders were two gentlemen, who were determined to keep close to their hearts, the possessions of their 'Angel' (Old Doc); who blessedly, had briefly 'walked among us'. But who were the two bidders? Yes, one bidder was Doc's son, Tomaso; he, sadly, had lost the bidding war due to lack of sufficient funds; he had wanted desperately to keep forever the jeep and his father's medical bag. It was, for Tomaso, a matter of love, and of honoring his father's memory

The second and winning bidder also wanted desperately to own the jeep and doctor bag, because 'Old Doc' had saved his child's life, and then, had refused payment.

The winning bidder then approached 'old Doc's' son, Tomaso, after the auction was over, and said, "Tomaso, I loved your father and I am so sorry that I caused you so much grief. Please forgive me; and with those words **he reluctantly, handed over the key** to Tomaso ---

The key of an 'old Angel's' Chariot;

And an old doctor's medical bag.

SO YOU WANT TO BE AN AUTHOR

Several years ago, I knew and worked with an individual who was truly, a, 'one of a kind'. Oh, he wasn't unique because of physical or mental prowess, he was just -- a normal ordinary man who lived and loved, like 'us all'; but, somehow, he was different. I guess he had that 'special something' which you can't see, but know that he has that 'IT', and that he 'is special'; I guess, he is what most folks would call a 'people's, 'people person'.

The individual I am telling you about was a Medical physician who loved what he was doing. He was not the smartest doctor in the world, but he seemed to always be able to make the right decision, and to timely arrive at the proper diagnoses. When he was asked "How did you know what that person's diagnosis was', he would innocently scratch his head, and say "heck, I don't know". Ah, but, **he did** know.

Early in his medical life (before the time of lawsuits, and all the other required documentation exams that are required to prove that a physician is a good doctor), he remained knowledgeable, lovable and, -- was simply, one of the best Doc's around. I suppose by this time you will be asking, what has all this to do with wanting to be an Author?

Patience, patience -- the answer will come, anon.

I believe it is good that there are required tests, and rules implemented, that safeguard the general population from unethical and unprepared health providers, but they do create additional stress for many members of the medical profession. How so, you might ask? Your question might be best answered by asking the following question. "Have you ever taken an examination that passing, or failing will determine your future livelihood"? There are several reasons why there is so much stress when taking medical examinations. Of course, one obvious reason is being unprepared; but, alas, there are some unfortunate individuals who simply cannot take an examination, because they become emotionally and mentally 'tied-up'; and then, all is lost!

Now, as promised, the answer to "why do you want to be an Author".

In earlier paragraphs, I had written a brief biography of a wonderful, knowledgeable physician; but what I didn't tell you, was, that he had failed the required Internal Medicine specialty competence examination; not just once -- but six times. Yes, he took the examination -- six years in a row, and failed the examination six times in a row, and then, in disgust, decided -- the heck with it -- no more exams.

But wait, when the seventh year arrived, and he didn't apply to take the test, the test sponsors actually entreated him to take the test one more time. Finally, finally, would you believe it, the number seven was his lucky number -- he did, finally, pass the test on his seventh try.

There was one remaining personal task for him to accomplish after passing the examination,

He **needed** to author a book -- and did so,

With the title --

HOW TO PASS A MEDICAL EXAMINATION

Of course, there are many reasons why folks do find the need to become Authors, but probably, there are only few reasons that are more compelling than that of our wonderful, perseverant 'man of medicine'. But *what are* the other reasons that compel, or prompt an otherwise normal individual to bare his/her soul for the world to see, and judge? The simple answer would be "You'd be surprised!

Of course, it is a well-established fact that the dissemination of knowledge via the written word is the hallmark of modern man; but the reasons for authorship are many. It is readily obvious, that without authorship of the many advances in Science, human experiences, and life's observations -- the human-race's legacy, as we know it, would soon be 'knowledge bankrupt'.

It should come as no surprise then, that the vast number of literary efforts are accomplished by the 'everyday, letter writing Authors'; i.e. those who write what their heart's and mind need to share with others. It seems that there are important human passions such as the need to be important, to be recognized, to 'make a buck', or to just fulfill a compelling need of promoting an idea; or promote a cause, are all common reasons for becoming an Author.

So, I guess, in the final analysis, we, all (me included), are, in one way or another, born to be Authors.

So, then, what attributes must one have to be an Author; and what rules, if any, must an Author observe? It would seem sensible to adhere to the same tenets that are required in 'every-day' living, i.e. always say plainly what you believe, and do so without rancor or animosity; and, remember, that what you scribe will be seen by many, and painfully, there will be few opportunities for later retraction of an ill-chosen word.

Sometimes, we write 'things' when our 'juices' are flowing mightily, so that what we think -- and write, are often accomplished at different speeds of brain and hand; so, that what was *intended* to be written wisely, will oft'time appear as disjointed hieroglyphics. Therefore, it is always wise to proof read -- before it is read by others and ridiculed -- as -- goofy-read!

The moral of this story is really quite clear; i.e., write what you *mean* to say, and do so within the bounds of thoughtfulness, and decency. Remember ---

What you have written, is not just ink spots on paper ---

It is a true reflection --

Of whom you are.

SOUPS ON!

The culinary art "ain't" what it used to be. Well, to be honest, it really isn't about the food itself that I'm referring to; it's <u>my</u> PRESENTATION of the food that sometimes causes me to have nightmares! Confused? Perhaps I should have mentioned that I am referring to a personal set of circumstances that occurs, twice a day, in a nursing home. I'll bet you're even more confused by now, so I'll quickly tell you the answer – by asking a question – "Have you ever tried to help feed a person who is afflicted with Alzheimer's disease, and if that person has no idea what a table utensil is?" Sadly, the story I am about to relate would be humorous, I suppose, if it were not so personally tragic in consequence. Yes, the story I am about to recount, is about the daily trials and tribulations encountered by my wife and me at lunch and suppertime dinning at the nursing home.

Approximately seven years ago, when my dear wife first exhibited early signs of her malady, there were rare instances of dinning-table misbehavior. Oh, I suppose you could consider eating a fresh ear of corn by the around and around, instead of the normal maneuver of eating from one end, to the other, a slightly abnormal behavior, but she ate her corn that strange way ever since we married, 63 years ago.

In recent years, while at home, she gradually progressed to a stage of dinning behavior that I would term –disorganized or, at best, fraught with irregularities; such as totally shunning dinning utensils, because she had no idea what they were, or what to do with them.

Now, and for the past three years in the nursing- home, lunch and dinner time have been, to say the least, stressful. There are times when she seems happy for me to be there for her, and willing to have me assists her with lunch and supper. There are other times, when she clams up like a Sphinx (Egyptian statue), and refuses all food or drink. However, when she does eat or drink fluids, the order of the day for the meal helper, is to have Patience, and to be vigilant, or else, the full dinner plate and liquids will suddenly be dispatched all over the table and floor. Oddly enough, when there is a "floor or table mishap" there is never a look of misgiving from her.

There are some tricks (maneuvers) that can be utilized by the caregiver (I've learned early on), that will help when she becomes a sphinx at meal time. Sometimes I will act as if it doesn't concern me if she eats or not; she will then, for some unknown reason gobble up all the food, as if there is no tomorrow. Another trick to induce her to eat is to actively and dramatically taste the food, but this ruse is rarely successful. If she refuses to eat for a day or more, I threaten to not come back for a while. I know that using threats is usually 'verboten', and probably should never be used; but it usually works if she is able to comprehend the meaning of your threat, AND, if you're being there is important to her; this last method to induce her to eat may work, at times, but it always causes great pain –TO ME!

Lastly, the words of the title "SOUPS ON" have great significance. Oh, sure, I could have titled this feckless story "BREAKING BREAD TOGETHER", or "MEAL TIME", OR, OR. But soups-on, at meal time, has made my job easier, and much more satisfying. Consider -- When she refuses to eat, and you are at your wits end, you have an "ace in the hole" – SOUP (like, soups on-- the menu)! She loves soup. Many times, when she refuses all foods presented to her, a spoonful of warm soup will open Pandora's - er -- her mouth, and then, all's well with the world.

Forgive me for making light of a very difficult and serious circumstance, but after many months, and thousands of daily stressful culinary events, this fatigued old warrior has only two choices – either laugh, or cry. I have chosen to make light of a very difficult situation; after all, isn't it well known that -

Old soldiers never cry -- on the -- outside.

THANK - YOU

How many times in your life have you said "thank-you"; and how many times have you heard the words "you're welcome"? Yes, saying 'thank you' has always been a conduit to a better 'something', and it, somehow, always makes me feel better to have acknowledged a kindness of a caring individual (or animal). But, what does thank-you, really mean? Oh, sure, a 'thank you' infers that it is something that you give, or do, to show thanks; it is a polite expression of gratitude. But, is that the end of the story? Of course not -- it is just the beginning!

Does thank-you, always mean 'thank you' i.e. is the meaning a sincere acknowledgement when receiving a physical, or personal gift, or service? The answer is: it all depends on the timing and inflection of the response. There have been many, many times that the 'thank - you' received, after having performed a "good deed," was either delayed, or worse -- it was a response in the tone of voice of the 'thank you,' that suggests -- a 'thank you' of --- I guess, oh humnn. But, happily, the majority of 'thank-yous' heard, are reflections of appreciation -- and, you are able to see the 'thank-you-sparkle', in their eyes.

Needless to say, there are many ways of saying thank-you, and there are many reasons to proclaim appreciation. Obviously, a thank-you expressed by a merchant, is vastly different in meaning and emotional content, than a thank-you expressed for saving a life. One of the most rewarding and pleasant memory for me, was a 'heartfelt 'thank-you' expressed from a patient who had recovered from a serious illness; and that, amazingly enough, was from a patient who rarely had a 'nice thing' to say, *about anything*. It is surprising how quickly one's attitude changes, when 'the shoe is on the other foot'! Ah, yes, it is always wise to say, thank-you, when appropriate, because, you never know 'what tomorrow will bring'.

I suppose it isn't always necessary to express appreciation by explicitly saying 'thank-you.' Of course, it's always nice to follow protocol and be polite, but sometimes, something more, should be offered to express just how important that "something done for you," was.

Yes, it was just a situation of importance, that prompted me to revisit the world of 'thank - yous' (thank–you / noun); plural -- (thank–yous) Merriam Webster Dictionary.

There are times, when thank yous are mandatory, even when 'that something,' was done for others, and not for you. Let me tell you a "little story" of kindness and duty. My little story may not seem that important to some folks, but --- to each his own I always say.

One morning, when I visited my Alzheimer's disease afflicted wife in the nursing home, as I do daily, to attend to her needs, and I was shocked to see that she had lost a frontal tooth. The reason for the tooth loss is another story for another time, but the pressing problem, was to get a dentist to attend to her misfortune. Aye, there's the rub, obtaining a dentist that is willing to come, to a "nursing home".

Fortunately, I thought, there would be a dentist who is contracted to come to her nursing home. And so, after considerable time and stress, "the" dentist" agreed to see her; but, alas, unbeknownst to me, the dentist's fee was to be paid in advance (a considerable amount). On the day of the appointment, the dentist refused to see her, when "the fee wasn't in his hand" prior to the consultation. So, what was I to do, what could I do?

Now, I will tell you the happy ending of my little story.

After considerable thought, I then called 'our Dentist' of many years, who practiced in another town, for his advice and perhaps the name of a Dentist that we could call. When he heard of my wife's dilemma, he instantly shouted "Why didn't you call me, I would come to see her". So, yes, he did come, not just once, but several times in the evening, even when I didn't know he had come, on his own, because he was concerned. And so, happily, ends a story of woe. But, hold on, could I end a story of such elegance, without comment? No, of course not,

I will now tell you -- the rest of the story.

I was well aware of the fact, that my wonderful dentist would not charge a fee commensurate with the value it represented to me, so I sent him a letter telling him how much I appreciated his caring and expertise, and demanded that he charge an adequate fee. However, I realized that he would never consider his efforts in a monetary way, so I included in the letter a $100 dollar debit card, with the following note:

Dear Doctor,

I want you to know how much I appreciate your caring, and expertise. It was terribly important to me that my wife's problem be taken care of quickly before it became worse. You have restored my faith in humanity, and are a credit to your profession. Please send me an adequate statement that will cover all your time and expertise.

Please accept this small token (debit card) of my affection and esteem. I know that a "Thank you" is the usual polite way of expressing gratitude;

But a Pastrami Sandwich --- is --- so much better.

The clock -- A CONTINUUM

This story of 'THE CLOCK,' is a story like no other. It is a story that transcends normal everyday reasoning; it is a story of a skilled, lonely Clock-maker, who had dedicated the last few years of his life to make a clock so beautiful and so precise, that the world would marvel, and gratefully accept his gift and remember him with honor, after he leaves this world of tears. His gift was so beautiful, that upon its completion he loving pressed it close to his bosom, and with great elation and tears in his eyes, softly exclaimed "Du bist mein schones kind" (You are my beautiful child)!

In the few short years following the completion of his masterpiece, the Clock, he, Oscar Schwartzenhaeger, enjoyed the deep love and companionship that existed between him and his 'son', the clock. There were days when he was sad -- and strangely enough, his "son" would also become sad, and 'his' chimes became listless and dull; and, when Oscar was happy, the clock's chimes were happy and melodic. Of course, to the casual passer-by, the changes noted in the chimes resonance were attributed to "atmospheric climate change"; Ah, but Oscar, KNEW, better!

Sadly, Oscar Schwartzanhaeger died peacefully at the age of 85, on the 10th of May, 1887 at 12:02 am, of age and fatigue. It was surprising, and baffling, to find, that Oscar's 'son' ('Schones kind') had suddenly stopped working at exactly 12:02 am, on the 10th of May. The people of the village thought that it was a strange occurrence, but assumed that it was 'just one of those things that happen in life'.

Upon Oscar's death, the village, in deep anguish, decided to place his muted 'masterpiece', The Clock, in the Town Hall for all to see and admire, and to forever remember their beloved "Oscar, the clock maker."

It was with great amazement, that Oscar's 'child` (The Clock), once again, began keeping precise time, and announced its awakening, with vibrant chimes, **at 12:02 am; precisely 1 week after the death of its `father`**. Why the clock stopped working for exactly the one week, will forever be a mystery. And so, yes, Oscar's 'legacy' continued for years thereafter by exuding its beauty, and proclaiming accurate time for all those who had loved and honored its 'father'.

Fantasy you say? How could an inanimate entity and a human being have a love affair, you ask? Is it possible? Perhaps -- perhaps; but please reserve your opinion until you have read the rest of the story.

Now, with your permission, part two --- The rest, of the story...

THE CLOCK -- A CONTINUUM.

Oscar Schwartzenhaeger was born on January 10, 1802, and was presented to the world by his proud parents, Heinrich and Hilda. Oscar was their third child, and had a brother, Karl, six years his senior; and a sister, Marlene, who was his idol later on in life, and was three years his senior. Oscar's home was in a tiny hamlet surrounded by the pastoral majesty of the Jura Mountain Range of Switzerland.

The Jura Mountain Range is located in the northwest corner of Switzerland and is the cradle of the Swiss watch making industry of today. Jura was the Celtic name given to the mountains because the range was much lower than the great Alps of central and southern Switzerland; and because, of the more hospitable climate of the lower elevation, these forests made possible the wonderful wood required to make the beautiful clock cabinets that were world-renowned.

Tragically, his brother, Karl, died early in life in a skiing accident, and his sister Marlene, left to pursue her own ambitions. Of course, Oscar chose to stay with his 'clock maker' father; and became a world renowned 'clockmaker'. Sadly, the law of nature, eventually claimed the lives of his mother, and devoted father.

Marlene, his sister, had moved to Bern, the Capital of Switzerland, to be an Artist, and had one son, Peter. As Peter grew up, Marlene would constantly tell him how beautiful, and how intricate, her Brother Oscar's clocks were, without realizing that her comments would profoundly influence young Peter's future course in life.

For the next many years, following Oscar's death, Marlene and her son, Peter (and later on, also, with Peter's son, Oscar), made annual pilgrimages to the tiny Hamlet where she and Oscar were born, to visit with old friends --- and to see Oscar's beautiful clock in the Hamlet's town Hall. Although everyone admired and praised the clock, *it was Peter's son, Oscar, who dearly loved that magnificent clock, and would stare at it in silence, with glazed eyes, for the longest time.*

It was the year, young Oscar turned sixteen that he and his Grandmother Marlene again visited her Hometown that destiny was to determine Young Oscar's future. As they were about to visit the village town hall to see Oscar's 'wonder clock', they were informed that Oscars exquisite timepiece had stopped working, and were chagrined to learn that the villagers were not going to have the clock repaired because they feared it might be permanently harmed by an incompetent repair person. It was then, at that movement, Young Oscar with tears in his eyes, softly pleaded, **"Please wait for me; I will repair it for you"**. He then turned to his Grandmother and pleaded "Please Grandmother, help me to become the best clock Maker in the world; I, **must be permitted to 'fix' my Great Uncle's beautiful clock."**

There was no doubt in anyone's mind that young Oscar would become a world-class clock-maker; because, it was said, 'destiny had willed it so'.

And, so it was, that 'young Oscar' eventually was permitted to repair the Hamlet's venerable 'work of art' --- the 'clock.' When advised that he could proceed with the clock repair, he exclaimed: *"I will restore my Uncle's 'Schones Kind' (beautiful child) to perfect health, God willing"!*

Although it did take many months to obtain the various rare springs, gears and special internal connections needed for the repair, the 'clock' was, at last, working magnificently; young Oscar announced "It will keep perfect time -- forever"; and after saying that, he, as did his Uncle before him, grasped the clock close to his bosom and whispered "Du bist

Ein schonest kind" (You are a beautiful child). The village people were ecstatic; they once again, had their ` "living treasure" -- Oscar's immortal gift -- 'the Clock'.

The days after its return to its place of honor in the village Town Hall, were `happy days`. It was truly an epiphany; it seemed as if Christmas had come early. The following days were blessed with the happy chimes of the clock as it announced the half-and-the hour, times of the day. **Then, on May 10, 12:02 am, the exact month, and exact time, that its father had died),** Oscar's 'child' suddenly stopped ticking; much to the dismay of the people of the village. Initially, it was thought that young Oscar had failed to do an adequate repair. But, after one week had passed, they realized that their assessment of Oscar's workmanship was incorrect, because, at **precisely at 12:02 am, exactly one week la**ter, the clock, once again resumed keeping perfect time, and extolling its happiness, with its glorious chimes.

Yes, the Clock, ('Mein Schones Kind,'

Had not forgotten to honor its father.

PS,

You have now read the story of The Clock. It is a narrative chronicling the love and emotional relationship between a clockmaker and his beautiful clock.

The question is once again queried? Is it possible for a human being and an inanimate entity, to have a loving and emotional relationship?

You be the Judge

THE DAY AFTER CHRISTMAS (DAY)

I guess all good things must end sometime, I'm told, but why is it that the good things in life always seem to end FASTER than the 'not so good things'? Heck, I don't know! Maybe it's that little twist of irony that we are heir to; and which, is probably also responsible for the torturously long delay that always occurs when we, as fifteen years-olds, can hardly wait to be sixteen so that we can get our driver's license (the kid's 'license' that our parents fear more than eating cauliflower).

Well, now, after enduring the tortuously *slow* days of waiting for `**THE DAY**`, *it had come, and unhappily, gone* – now what? Sure, the day after Christmas still lingers with an aura of 'something special' is in the air, and we still walk around just a little lighter-of-foot; but down deep, there is a feeling that something isn't quite right – sort of like the sensation that one has when there is a lost prized possession, or when a dear friend had left for a short period of time; there is a vague sadness. Oh, yes, one knows that things will probably get better, and understands that the friend will return; and, so too, that the 'lost' possession may have only been misplaced, but --- --.

If you are a child, the excitement of the season, and the joy of having "I got just what I always wanted" is still center stage; the post-Christmas depression is postponed for a period of time – usually to a time when the return to school's 'horror time', is imminent. But, the deep feeling of depression is spontaneously averted once their daily activities of school, life's needs, and friendships had short-circuited depression's fearsome tentacles.

Ah, but what about the poor souls who had awaited the arrival of their Savior, and were reverently hoping and praying for a miracle (a merciful hand from God) that would help them remove the shackles of desolation, and despair, that had enslaved them? Yes, their only hope for deliverance had seemingly vanished, but perhaps, perhaps, there was still hope; maybe a prayer -- just maybe, they had not been forgotten – the Lord works in mysterious ways; but, sadly, depression may still persist.

Happily, for most of us, the Christmas holiday with all its cheer, tinsel and comradery and felicity, *had given us a deeper sense of spirituality*. It reaffirmed our bonds of kindred- ship, and fellowship with our fellowman; it made the world around us just a little kinder and better (at least for a time).

Although the spirit, and love of Christmas and its wonderful significance persists for a time, there soon looms distractions that cause uneasiness – ah, yes, distractions that must be attended to rather quickly – the Christmas season DEBT! It's true that love has no bounds during extreme emotion, and that we tend to `go overboard` in expressing our love and felicity, but it's also true that love and generosity can oft 'times be expensive. I wouldn't categorize `bill-paying` as a cause for depression, rather, I would say, it imparts a state of worried remorsefulness that sooner or later disappears, and tranquility once more returns – providing, due vigilance had been exercised

Although, the feelings of love and contentment are still manifest the day, and days, following the Christmas Day and Christmas season, they, the warm emotions and experiences of Christmas, have been subconsciously secreted away into our memories and souls. *And, yes, it is those warm memories of love and caring that sustain us throughout the year.* Remarkably, it is those warm feelings and emotions, that *have incrementally and gradually, year by year, constructed barriers to protect us against the untoward circumstances that are constantly attempting to undermine our tranquility and happiness.*

So, yes, Christmas Day, the day after Christmas, and
the succeeding three hundred sixty five days of the
year, are inseparable conduits; permitting ---

A continuum of Christmases' love – and is ---

A safeguard of our souls.

THE EASTER BASKET HUNT

Easter, and *its true significance*, has always been celebrated by the Christian World with the greatest reverence and love for over 2000 years.

Easter, has been celebrated by me, for only 88 years, and the Easter Basket hunt has been, for me, one of the most endearing, awaited "ritual" of the Easter season; it's sort of like Christmas, only better! Oh, don't misunderstand; I love the Christmas Holiday season too, and for the same reason – *its true significance,* but somehow or other, Easter with its Easter Basket hunt, and its delicious rewards – is so much SWEETER.

I suppose the celebration of Easter, and the Christmas Holiday seasons have much more significance for the older generations, because their lives were severely impacted by the Great Depression of the 20's and 30's; poverty with all its horrible baggage, was the norm. So, celebrating the arrival of Our Messenger of love at Christmas Time, and His resurrection at Easter time, gave great hope and courage to all who were suffering. With His arrival, at Christmas time, and return from the dead, at Easter time – *things would surely **have** to get better.*

But, what about the Easter basket hunt?

I will first tell you about **my** Easter Basket hunts over the past many years, and then tell you, anon, how the Easter Basket hunt came into being.

I alluded to the fact that Easter, for me, was a "sweeter" holiday than the Christmas holiday. Well, consider a moment. During the late 1920's and the mid- 30', the depression was in full bloom, and the usual "stocking fillers" were inexpensive hardtack cookies, hardtack candy, an orange, or a small toy if you were lucky. Ah, but Easter time was so much more "candy – better"! Of course, we didn't get many toys for Easter, but we always got Jelly beans, the crème-de-la crème of the "sweet-world"! I remember, one Easter, the Easter Bunny even brought me a large chocolate coated, gooey filled egg-shaped delicious morsel – it even had my name boldly scrolled across it, with gobs of yummy icing.

The Easter basket hunt was another matter! As I remember, the Easter baskets were fairly easy to find when we were small, although even then, finding the Easter basket under the waste paper basket in the closet, took some time to find. Later, as we became worldlier, the baskets on Easter morning were so well camouflaged, or hidden, that many times it required help from the Easter bunny's surrogates to find them.

There was one Easter morning that will forever be remembered by me, as, "the invisible Easter basket Morning". That particular Easter day was warmer than many previous Easters, so the Easter bunny had many more hiding places to conceal the baskets. In my favor, however, I had had several years' experience as an Easter basket sleuth, and was considered one of the best "Easter basket gumshoe" in the business.

When the search for the Easter basket commenced that Easter morning, I confidently looked into the usual places, and into the less common places, where previous baskets had been secreted; but, alas, without success. By this time, an hour had passed, and I, who had been "lightheartedly looking," began to search in earnest. After several more hours without success, the search was ended; I could not find the missing "invisible Easter basket!" It was only when, in defeat, I had raised the white flag of surrender, that the Easter Bunny's surrogates directed me to my "invisible" Easter basket.

I, to this day, am still smarting about that fateful Easter morning. If only I had heeded the weather man's warm weather forecast, I probably would have thought about – the, then, cold coal furnace in the cellar, as being the hiding place, and would have thought to look into its deepest, innermost confines; because there, partially masked by a few large lumps of coal, would have found my Easter basket! Oh, the pain!

Now, as promised, the origin of the Easter basket hunt, and **other Easter stuff.**

Easter Hare

The Romans believed that all life proceeded from an egg, so the egg came to symbolize birth and rebirth. Christians regarded eggs as the seeds of life and attributed them with the symbol of Jesus' resurrection.

The rabbit was used in early Easter celebrations to symbolize fertility, perhaps because these animals give birth to multiple offspring at a time. Anglo-Saxon mythology says that Ostara (goddess in Germanic paganism) changed her pet bird into a rabbit to entertain a group of children, and the rabbit laid brightly colored eggs for them.

Easter was once celebrated by giving colored eggs to children and later evolved to hiding them in the grass, where they had supposedly been laid by a hare. Children referred to this Easter mascot as the "Easter Hare," which later became known as the "Easter Bunny."

Easter Bonnet

When Christians adopted Easter, they paired this festival of springtime with a sermon. Following the tradition of dressing up for church, Easter Sunday became a special occasion to wear your very best clothes. In fact, many regarded Easter as the first time to wear a new dress and "Easter bonnet". In the early 1900's families would stroll to church and home again on Easter to show off their "Sunday best."

Easter Basket

The Easter basket evolved from a Catholic tradition, where each family brought a basket of food to mass on Easter Sunday to have it blessed for the evening meal. Later, children would use Easter baskets to gather colored eggs and candy.

Aristotle

THE FOUR PICTURE STORY

Someone once said "Pictures reveal the very essence of our souls" -- perhaps, perhaps! But, in truth, the four pictures I am about to reveal to you, are truly, in essence, responsible for the continuing health – of my soul!

It seems that there is a guiding hand that appears when one is lost and knows not what to do. It seems that what we do in life, and how we conducted our affairs, are not just random acts of spontaneous behavior, but are carefully planned by some 'meticulous entity' who had "planned it all".

Not too many 'moons' ago, I had written a heartbreaking story titled "AN ENDURING LOVE AFFAIR". I began the story by writing: "It was in September that I met an angel. It was in September, mid twentieth century, that I, a moth, was drawn towards the flame that has imparted warmth, kept me safe and nurtured me for the past sixty-three years – a flame that I call, wife". It is a story that had required every fabric of courage that I possessed to write it. It is a story about when I met her, loved her, and, sadly, lost her, to an enemy that has no mercy. The enemy, known as Alzheimer's disease, has gradually, and relentlessly stolen her mind, and ravaged her body; but it is abundantly clear that even after many, many months of attack, the flame, HER flame, that had seared my soul, is ever burning brightly within her—it cannot, and will not, ever be extinguished!

During the following months, no, years, spent with her on a daily basis caring and loving her, age and demoralization have taken their toll. It is the realization that there is no cure for her, and that it was no longer a question of "if", it is only a question of "when" that causes me the most pain.

It was during this period of desolation, that an epiphany occurred, that instantly changed my life for the better – it was an old, abandoned wallet that appeared, seemingly, out of nowhere; but it wasn't the weathered, torn wallet that caused me such shock; it was the three images that were faded, torn, and long forgotten pictures of my Angel, found nestled within its loving folds. It was a therapeutic potion, administered by the hand of fate, just when all appeared lost. It's amazing how bright and beautiful they were, even though sixty four long years had passed in silence since they were taken. There, in front of me, appeared visions that were real, not memories. There, in my hand, were my angel's images that I had seen so many times these past many years, only in my dreams. Yes, it was truly a dream come true, for me.

The pictures brought back a flood of wonderful memories. How is it that I, an eighty-eight year old codger, can remember the exact moment that the pictures were taken by my box camera, so many years ago (1950), and not be able to tell you what was eaten at breakfast? Nevertheless, I remember saying to her, as she was sitting relaxed on a towel, on the banks of the Olentangy River – SCHMILE please. And, how could I ever forget taking that picture of her, in graduation cap and gown, documenting her success of graduating from Ohio State University in 1950, with a degree in Bacteriology. I suppose the picture would have been more impressive if it had not been taken in the Ohio State University parking lot, but what the heck, I was so proud of her. Lastly, the picture of me, and my dear wife, taken in 1954, was especially soul satisfying; it was taken while on a brief vacation after my graduation from the Ohio State University School of Medicine. It was a vacation, and a reward for having suffered four long years of hard school effort and deprivation.

And, so – after three tumultuous years ---

We had passed our first major challenge as life-partners; it served notice to all, that we were an unbeatable team, and that we were capable to best, and survive, all adversities; we recently managed to reach our 64rd wedding anniversary --- and, yes, we are still counting – and will continue to count ---

UNTIL DEATH, DO US PART

Now, you have read my chronicle of 'The four picture story'; it is a narrative of love that transcends time. Yes, the past many yesterdays and the todays, do seem to have amalgamated into a seamless continuum for me; nothing has changed for me. The love and caring of yesteryears, remains constant today; it is only the faded, black and white images, recently found, that belie the fact that sixty four years have passed unnoticed.

I know that the images appearing on the following pages are faded, grainy and ill-disposed, but they are so beautiful to me.

The Pictures

1) Relatively recent portrait of my Angel and me
2) Graduation – 1950 Degree in Bacteriology
3) Celebration - Graduation – 1954 Doctorate degree
4) My Angel, when first we met- 1950

THE GREEN-EYED MONSTER

Green is a color in the spectrum of visible light located between blue and yellow. It is evoked by light with a predominant wavelength of roughly 495—570nm.

Now that we know facts about the beauty of nature, what did Shakespeare mean when he employed the expression "Green-eyed Monster" that was written in Othello?

The green-eyed monster In *Othello*, 1604, Shakespeare also alludes to cats as green-eyed monsters in the way that they play with mice before killing them.

Iago:
"O, beware, my lord, of jealousy;
It is the green-ey'd monster, which doth mock
The meat it feeds on. That cuckold lives in bliss,
Who, certain of his fate, loves not his wronger:
But O, what damnèd minutes tells he o'er
Who dotes, yet doubts, suspects, yet strongly loves!"

Othello:
O misery!

Othello Act 3, scene 3, 165–171

"The notion that jealousy is green-eyed is probably older than Shakespeare, although Shakespeare is our earliest authority in print. In *The Merchant of Venice,* Portia refers to "green-eyed jealousy" (Act 3, scene 2), and here Shakespeare coins the more intense phrase "green-ey'd monster." Renaissance Englishmen often paired colors with emotions or personal qualities: both green and yellow are emblematic of jealousy and green is also emblematic of envy" e.g., "she was green with envy"

"The basic idea is that the fortunate man *knows* his wife is cheating; the unfortunate man only *suspects* it, and is caught between the jaws of affection and anxiety. History and Shakespeare's infinity of cuckold (husband with adulterous wife) jokes, testify that Renaissance men were particularly prone to suspect their wives. The social perils of cuckoldry were severe indeed: it ruined a man's credit and debased his wife. Such consequences produced an advanced state of jealous suspicion known as "horn-madness," named after the metaphorical horns that were supposed to sprout from the cuckold's brow".

Bing Dictionary

I honestly am not sure why I decided to write about the base human emotions, of jealousy and envy, at this late stage of my life. I guess **the devil made me do it!** I assume that I and most other red-blooded human beings, have had, or will have, an encounter with the perils of jealousy or envy during their lifetime. Unfortunately, those of us who have experienced such emotions are so much the poorer for the encounters. It seems that these two emotions, jealousy and envy, are tragically woven so deeply into the basic fabric of our being that finding a cure, or a remedial potion to lessen the inevitable resultant pain, is nonexistent.

Although jealousy and envy are often discussed as one emotion, there are differences of major proportions, in their meaning. Simply put, *to be envious* -- is to covet something – that you "ain't" got, but would like to have e.g., to have a sensuous body like the blond girl next door. On the other hand, *to be jealous* -- is to have something you possess and cherish threatened or taken away e.g., like losing your husband to that gorgeous blond next door! Of course, the two emotions are often painfully intertwined.

What then? If there is no cure, or remedial solution for these unearthly, poisonous emotions that exist between Heaven and Hell, what then? How would it be possible to change, or ameliorate, such deep seated emotions (jealously and envy) that are seemingly shackled to our very Souls? The only conceivable answer lies within each person's genome; in brief, we are all (mentally and physically endowed) whence (from where) we came. It is only when we realize that the emotions of jealousy and envy are self-destructive, that some measure of change is possible. Or, put another way, "To oneself be true". As is true of most untreatable maladies, prevention assumes greater importance. In many diseases, vaccines and changes in life style and behavior have proven to be of great value. But alas, there are no vaccines, or changes of life style or behavior that could possibly offer a cure. No, the only salvation lies in the education of one's self.

Although an education will not give you a beautiful, or powerful body, it may allow you to master, one, or another, field of expertise that may give you great pleasure, self-esteem and, perhaps, recognition. Thus, when an individual is pleased with him/herself, the need or desire to emulate others (be envious) fades into thin air; and the fear of rejection and loss (jealousy), evades an uncomfortable memory.

PS,

I must reluctantly report that Shakespeare's 17th century Green- eyed monster is still alive and kicking, today.

THE IMPORTANCE OF
BEING IMPORTANT

There is one word in the English Language that always puzzles, and at the same time, mesmerizes me; and that word is "Important" (significant, vital, imperative, central, main etc.). I have no idea why the word puzzles me, since I know that the word suggests someone or something is presumed to be "better" (stands out from the ordinary), but I really have no clue as to _what is_ the true meaning of the word. If the meaning implies something or someone is 'special', I still have no idea of the degree, or the reason for that special allusion.

From my earliest remembrances, and even today, I seem to have a vague sense of urgency and excitement when I hear "Now pay attention, _this is important_" or, when I am told, "Now, _this is more important_ than you think." When I was growing-up, I heard that "I-p" word so often I began to think -- important -- _wasn't important!_

Later-on in life, I began to realize that there are many nuances i.e. shades, tones, distinctions, tinges, tints and touches of the word, 'Important'. After many years of struggle e.g., I graduated from Medical School, and subsequent postgraduate training, and I became an "IMPORTANT" Medical Doctor – or, so I thought; little did I realize how wrong that assumption was... I had confused presumed excellence, with _being_ important. But, as it turned out, I was neither excellent, nor important. _Ah yes, the combination of youth and inexperience are at times burdensome, and can only be cured by ageing (maturing) and spending time on the job (experience)._

Upon graduation (from any higher education facility) it isn't unusual to see newly minted young stalwarts strutting around with new-found self-importance (as well they should, to some degree) but, if they are lucky, wisdom will soon permeate their world with life's realities; they will soon learn that their new-found wisdom is only "skin deep", and it will take a lifetime of continuous learning and effort to possibly attain their goal of being -- 'important'?

I remember, only too well, the Euphoria I experienced when I finally graduated from Medical School, and passed the required State Medical Board examination that permitted me to practice medicine in the State of Ohio – *I <u>Knew</u> I was one of the best (important) Doc's around. But, alas, those many hard years of scholastic effort and brash youth, had caused my temporary insanity – I later, unhappily, reasoned.*

THE TRUE REALITY

The following 15 years of medical practice were bitter/sweet for me. I loved what I was doing, and tried desperately to keep up with the rapid advances in medical knowledge but was dismayed to learn, that try as I may, I would never be able to keep up with the vast changes in medical science. Worse yet, much of my earlier learned medical truisms, were later found to be suspect. In addition, the result of the increased stress of my large medical practice and, sadly, the stress of increasing patient adversarial behavior, had a profound psychological impact on me. Thus, I began to feel threatened, and less 'important' (needed); I began to question my medical competency, and will to continue.

So, by the 15th year of practice, I had lost all thoughts of being 'important,' or of being, a good doctor.

As the years passed, I continued my practice, and fatefully attempted to keep up with the burgeoning mass of new knowledge, and the ever changing stressful medical milieu.

By the 25th year of practice, I continued to feel uncomfortable, about whom I was as a Doctor, but I also began to realize that although I would never know all there is to know, I did, gradually, understand how much -- **I didn't know**.

By the 30th year of practice, I finally had decided that I would continue trying to keep abreast of new developments, as best I could, and honestly do the best job possible. *I, at last, was mostly comfortable with myself, and my profession.*

Perhaps, my medical life's experiences were different than many other physicians', or maybe I was just a slow learner – if so, so be it. It is of interest though, that now, the trend in medical practice is to concentrate on narrower areas of expertise; there is simply too much knowledge for one person to embrace and master.

Finally, a few thoughts: There is a vast difference between being important because of your accomplishments and / or contributions, and of being important just because *you* say, *you* are important. Obviously, the "self-important" individual has serious personal issues e.g., I remember an incident that occurred while in Medical School that caused me to seriously re-evaluate my own place in life.

One day, I and other students were observing a skilled surgeon perform a very difficult surgical procedure. He accomplished the needed medical corrections with great skill but, alas, he revealed a major personality flaw. After he had just masterfully closed the huge wound, one of the observing medical students complimented the surgeon by saying "Sir, that wound came together, beautifully"! The surgeon quickly turned on the student, and in a harsh tone said, "Son, that wound didn't come together – I PULLED IT TOGETHER!!

> *Yes, the importance of being important – is (for good or*
> *bad) an important facet of the human condition.*

PS,

Admonition – Proclaimed Self-importance (arrogant or pompous behavior), may be dangerous to your health!

THE LIFE AND LOVES OF JAZZY

The world has just lost a tiny speck of sunshine that had brightened many lives, and softened the harsh everyday burdens of all living souls who knew and loved you; you, Jazzy, our four legged bundle of canine joy, gave us unconditional love without asking for anything other than a little attention, caring and sustenance.

Jazzy

How best can you, a wondrous 'ball of happiness' be described? Would saying that you were sent to us, by the 'Great Lover of all creatures,' large and small, to fill our hearts with joy and contentment be sufficient? Yes! Your love has helped us through many stressful times, and lovingly provided solace, when we were in deep despair.

How will it be possible to ever forget the happy days of seeing you playing in the swimming pool, or throwing yourself into a mound of snow, or chasing snowflakes that were falling all around you?

Jazzy, the whole world will miss your loving grace. You have fought a courageous battle against superior, malignant forces, and lost, but you were valiant to the end.

You will surely be missed by those of us who were fortunate enough to know and love you. It is the will of God that you leave our home, but you will never, ever, leave our hearts and minds.

All living creatures must follow the dictates of nature; we, all, are temporary candles that flame, slowly flicker, and then at an appointed hour, must pass away.

So, dear friend, farewell; may you forever rest in peace.

We will sadly miss you, but know ---

It is better to have loved you, and lost;

Than not to have known and loved you at all

THE LOVE STORY

Have you ever been in Love; if so, would you please tell me what LOVE is? I have spent countless hours, over a life span of 88 plus years, trying to find the answer. I know that the dictionaries tell us that the synonyms of love are: darling; dear; sweetheart; honey etc., but none of the words tell us WHAT love is. So, in the following paragraphs, I will attempt to tell you what I have gleaned (collected) from the literature, and from much wiser folks than me. It seems to me that the word, love, is commonly used (perhaps, too commonly) in everyday parlance, when a better choice of word would be more appropriate, e.g. "I *like* eggs", would be more in keeping with reality than saying "I *love eggs*" -- but, anyway, it's good, that eggs are included in the diet.

For these past many years, the word, CARING, has been FOR ME, the only word that most closely conveys the meaning of the word, LOVE.

Now, my story, `THE LOVE STORY`

But what is love? The answer should have been surmised, when we realize that it was the same superb Creator who had fashioned us with an immense, exquisite system of electrical and chemical mediators that control our every thought, and seamlessly, control all aspects of our lives. It is no surprise, then, that *love is a chemical state of mind*; and the feelings that we experience when we fall in love, are similar to a true addiction, that are mediated by the same chemical reactions. Romantic love exhilarates and motivates us; and the chemicals that permeate our brain are essential determinants, that guarantee the continuation of our species. It is the power of these chemicals that make us want, and raise children.

We know that romantic love is a true emotion, regardless of culture, or country, but differences do exist on how love is displayed.

How and why do we fall in love; what makes us fall in love? Interestingly, a Professor Aron, of State University conducted an experiment to learn what happens when people fall in love, and found that simply staring into each other's eyes, has tremendous impact. He put *strangers* of the opposite sex together for 90 minutes and had them discus intimate details about themselves, and then had them stare into each other's eyes for four minutes without talking. The results? Many felt a deep attraction for their partner after the experiment, and two even ended up getting married six months later.

The existences of animal pheromones (excitement carriers), are individual 'scent' prints found in urine and sweat that dictate sexual behavior, and attract the opposite sex. This odorless chemical helps animals select and choose mates with immune systems that **are different** than their own -- and thus ensure healthy offspring. Human pheromones were discovered, in urine, in 1980 by scientists at the Chemical Senses in Philadelphia and its counterpart in France.

It appears that we all have a template for the ideal partner secreted in our subconscious, and it is that love map that decides which person in this, whole wide world around us, will catch our eye. And, yes, that template may be formed by the appearance of the opposite sex, who remind us of our parents, friends -- or even, remind us, in a vailed sort of way, *of our own likeness* (picture, picture on the wall, who is the fairest of them all?)

Smell is an important part of love. An experiment was conducted where a group of females smelled the unwashed tee shirts of a group of sweaty males, and each had to select the one to whom she was most attracted. The majority of the females chose a shirt from the male who's IMMUNE SYSTEM WAS MOST UNLIKE THEIR OWN.

> Sexologist John Money's definition of 'lust' and love; "Love exists above the belt, lust below; love is lyrical, lust is lewd"; *it is the lust that keeps us looking, but it is the predetermined desire for love and romance, that leads us to attraction.*

But, what is all this talk about chemicals? How do chemicals fit in the 'love picture'? Yes, it can be said that love IS a series of chemical reactions, i.e. the hormones, estrogen and testosterone, are the introducing agents that beckon the opposite sex, but if they were absent, there would be very few "sexual" encounters --with the opposite sex. Ah, but once there is an encounter with the opposite sex, Dopamine arises to produce love's loving bliss -- it is our 'pleasure agent; ' and happily, Dopamine is then joined with an agent, Norepinephrine, to excite us, and race our hearts; -- and together, produce loves intense energy, elation, sleeplessness, excitement, loss of appetite, and all sorts of goofy wonderful feelings.

We should not forget one other chemical that also plays an important role in the attraction stage of love. Apparently the levels of Serotonin, the mediator of our neural circuits that are responsible for how we assess others, *are lowered*, and thus we see lovers obsess about their partner's perfect virtues, and nary a wart would / could, they ever see.

The final stage of a love relationship is attachment and commitment. If the commitment is strong, and is felt by both of them -- the attachment is long enduring. Oft'time, the 'romantic passion' (when we lose the ability to think rationally) eventually subsides, we begin to see the warts of our 'perfect amour, ' that we were not able to see during the passion period, that trouble might begin. It is that time of the relationship that will determine whether or not it will be an enduring successful attachment, or failure. *If the relationship is based on mutual caring, respect, and friendship, a long term commitment is the reward. So, yes,*

LOVE -- IS -- CARING

PS,
Caring,
  The commitment, and the need to protect, keep safe from harm and deprivation; and are done so, in a compassionate and loving way.

THE PASSAGE OF TIME

There was a time in my life that I thought time was, well, `time`; there was never a reason to question, or even think, about what `time` was. Oh, sure, I knew that it was time to eat, or it was time to go -- and that `was it`. But now, I find that some folks have `interesting thoughts` about the difference of, and between, past and present, `time`. I will not even try to understand the enormous amount of `thoughts` about `time relativity` expressed in the published encyclopedia of Philosophy (2000); but in that discussion -- `The nature and Experience of Time`, found in autobiographical `Confessions of St Augustine" (354 AD), were discussed.

At the age of 32, St Augustine wrote, in Book XI, the following: "when we say that an event or interval is short or long, what is it that is being described as of short or long duration? It cannot be what is past, since it has ceased to be, and what is non-existent cannot presently have any properties, such as being long. But neither can it be what is present, for the present has no duration; his answer to this puzzle? "What we are measuring, when we measure the duration of an event or interval of time, *is in the memory -- therefore: his conclusion -- `the past and future exist only in the mind`.*

Well, now, we now know why there is no REAL past or future -- don't we? I have to admit -- his reasoning sure does make sense?? I suppose *it does make sense,* if you're a PSYCHOANALYST (A Sigmund Freud `thing`). However, unless someone tells me different, I DO have a REAL past, since I am now well beyond the eighty-year mark (of living), and my body is telling me (with aches and pains) that accomplishing that feat of living a long life was a real `tough` event, and was not a figment of my imagination.

No kidding though, St Augustine was obviously a learned man, and knew the difference between fantasy and reality; he was merely trying to explain that `time` has no borders`; `time` is -- well, `time`, and can only be accessed by `thinking about it` as, a, `here today, gone tomorrow,` event -- there is no other way to define, or categorize, THE PASSAGE OF TIME.

When I began this hapless discussion, I remarked: "There was a time in my early life that I thought time was, well, just 'time'. There was never a reason to question, or even think, about what 'time' was. Oh, sure, I knew that it was time to 'study', **or it was time to go -- and that 'was it'; but, what I didn't tell you, was that the** 'time puzzle' (riddle), has been my 'waterloo' (to encounter one's ultimate obstacle, and to be defeated by it)"; but, in more recent times, I had even attempted to write a story, titled "TIME", that chronicled my exercise in, 'time - futility'.

But, tempus fugit, so instead of confusing you even more, I would like to share with you a little 'time game' that I have been playing for many years; even before I knew there was an individual named St. Augustine (354 AD). If you recall, St Augustine's conclusion about 'time' was: -- **the past and future exist only in the mind.** Ah, yes, MY 'time game' IS, a '**mind**'-time game. Let me tell you the 'rules' of my private game. Firstly, you must be relaxed, and ready for a good night's sleep; yep, that's it. Ah, but, when you awaken from sleep --THAT'S, when this 'quirky, interesting 'time-game' commences. Let's be clear, there can be no 'hanky-panky' (cheating) played at this time; you must sit on the edge of your bed, and, **before looking at the clock,** state clearly, the exact time that you **think, is, the current time.** I know, you probably think this is just a silly guessing game played by a senile old man, but really, not so! Consider: If St. Augustine's hypothesis is correct, then, thinking does make it so. And, if one considers all the facts, such as: Do I feel rested; is it still dark outside; do I hear the school bus, or cars, on the road; are the birds singing, and do I have an urgent need for the comfort station, are all *mental determinants* required to give you, a '**time sense**'. So, if the thinking cap is on straight, and, if your perceptive power switch is turned on ---Voilà, you should be -- **right on,** the time -- **sometimes?**

This morning, I was off by four minutes!

St Augustine was correct,

The past and future do exist, but only, in the mind.

PS

Tempus fugit is a <u>Latin phrase</u>, usually translated into <u>English</u> as "**time flies**". The expression comes from line 284 of book 3 of <u>Virgil</u>'s *<u>Georgics</u>*,[1] where it appears as *<u>fugit inreparabile tempus</u>*: "it escapes, irretrievable time". The phrase is used in both its Latin and English forms as a <u>proverb</u> that "time's a-wasting". *Tempus fugit*, however, is typically employed as an admonition against sloth and procrastination (cf. *<u>carpe diem</u>*) rather than a motto in favor of licentiousness (cf. "<u>gather ye rosebuds while ye may</u>"); the English form is often merely descriptive: "time flies like the wind", "time flies when you're having fun". --- Wikipedia

See, I knew there was more to time, than being only in the mind.

THE REDEYED DRUMMER

Let me ask the question "What has red eyes, emerges from a long sleep and appears suddenly via an `earth` chimney, and then, proceeds to quickly drive us crazy with its cacophonous (jarring, disharmonious) drum-beating sound? Not sure of the answer? Well then, what if I added that shortly after `emerging into view` they, *appearing* to be naked, quickly find a tree or a similar structure, take off their skins (ecdysis -molting), and proudly reveal their two pairs of membranous wings. Still not sure of what I am describing? Oh, I know, you would know the correct answer, for sure, if I had added that our red eyed drummer had, in addition to their prominent (.8 -2") compound eyes, three `simple` eyes. **Of course**, --- it is our `13 or 17` year insect, -- the **CICADA**. We old-timers always called them --- LOCUST; but, in 44 other different languages of the world, our Red eyed musician is named: Zikade (German); Tzitziki (Greek); Cicala (Italian); Greier (Romanian); And, Cha`n (Chinese), etc., etc.

So, as you can see, we have a World celebrity in our midst, and which periodically appears, *at different times of the year, all over the world.*

Yes, *our* little drummers also appear in our locality in Ohio, on a somewhat lengthy intermittent schedule; i.e. the specie viii appeared in -- 1951; 1968; 1985; 2002. To be sure, there is always an exception to the rule for the 13, and 17 year arrivals times -- for instance, there is a species of cicada that does appear only on a yearly basis; but the vast majority of Cicada remains in their subterranean cocoons 13 to 17 years before emerging. However, depending on the species and location, many 17 year `stragglers` may appear 1 - 4 years early; and some of the 13 year `stragglers` may appear 1- 4 years late.

Well, no matter; whether they are the 13 or 17 year visitors, they *all will appear* in the springtime when the temperature of the earth (8 inches below the surface) is 64 degrees. If one would look carefully, you would easily find the earthen `chimney` from which our little Cicada (nymphs) will emerge to do what little nymphs do -- and do so, frantically -- they procreate! Consider: They emerge, proceed to rapidly molt, and then feverishly begin their calling, and searching, for a mate without even pausing to eat.

Since there is no assurance of the exact date of our redeye drummer's next arrival, I would like to briefly tell you `*how it was,* ` when the cicada last invaded North East Ohio in June, 2002. The following few paragraphs are from an article I had written in mid-June, 2002, titled `AN UNUSUAL YEAR.'

`First, I wonder how many people still remember the past "cicada phenomena" that was "once upon" us in 1985? Well, it is now mid-June 2002, and we are now blessed, once again, with a visit from our subterranean friends, the cicada. I know that if you had experienced (and remembered) the sights and sounds of that last "invasion" of the cicada seventeen years ago, you will probably do what I, and many others will do -- we will shrug, smile, grimace, and just relax, because we know they won't be here forever (it will just *seem, to* last forever)!

And, yes, you will smile when you remember how the grandchildren played "Star wars" with the shells (nymphal cases); and, yes, you will smile as you see your very special feline playing with the "shells", thinking they are a fun toy, and alas, shrug when you see people eating them (as in a Cicada pizza pie)!! Lastly, you will grimace when you see your dog or cat eating them, and hope that *everything* will *come out,* alright.

The cicada announces their arrival by using their drum-like membranes on the side of the abdomen. The resulting cacophony (harsh, jarring, dissonant sounds) that results in an unforgettable sound that travels in waves for great distances, as these strange "bugs" go in search of a mate.

Over the years, I have remembrances of painful bites caused by black flies, mosquitoes and other "bugs" that seem to find great delight in causing pain. I can remember thinking at those times, that somehow or other, there had to have been a miscalculation (mistake!) in the CREATION scenario! Surely, there could not be a plausible reason for their existence (for the black flies, mosquito), since their whole reason for being, is to bite and cause pain and disease; but what do I know?

On the other hand, the Cicadae are merely nuisance "bugs". They crunch when you step on them, cling to your clothes, hair etc. but they DO NOT BITE, for which, I am grateful.

The upside (for us) is that they will die in two to four weeks, and their progeny will go underground and not return for another seventeen years. So I guess we can tolerate a little noise (squishing or cacophony) for a little while.

I could not help but wonder how, I, would respond, if I were placed in a similar circumstance as the Cicada. Think of it: they emerge, proceed to rapidly molt, then feverishly begin their call and search for a mate without pausing to eat. But, considering the very short time allotted to them for their life cycle, their sequence of activity *is surely, reasonable!! After all, first things first, I always say.* And so, no matter how you feel about these critters, whether you call them "bugs", locust, or cicada, they will soon leave (one way or another). They will then return in seventeen years (or so) for a repeat performance --- orchestra, fanfare and all!!

To be honest, I will look forward to their "miracle" return in seventeen years, and will enjoy their cacophonous medley once again` ---

Really?

THE RELUCTANT HEALER

Things happen!

How is it that we, as a Human race, have no control over our futures, or what we do in life? Why can't we assert ourselves and say "enough, it's my life, I should be able to determine the direction and pathway I WILL follow"! But, it's an idle question; most of us eventually realize that we do what we do – it's our destiny! Fortunately, when it's all said and done, most of us are able to say "Heck, I'm kind of proud of what I did in life, after all, what else could I have done better?" And so it was for Paul de Zuse, our reluctant Healer; he fought his way, reluctantly – into immortality.

Life, for Paul de Zuse, early on, was pleasant enough. His father, a well-known, capable physician loved him, and his two brothers and sister very much. Some would say that his father was too strict with the children, but he desperately wanted to safeguard their lives and futures, so he, perhaps, tried too hard. It wasn't too unusual to hear him say to the children" I don't care what you do in life – as long as you become physicians!" Needless to say, the children responded to this constant reminder of what their future will be, with rebellious frustration – there would, in no way, be a chance in h-- that they would become physicians!! Their mother, Marie, on the other hand, was a gentle soul who understood her husband's harsh love, and her children's rebellion, so she became a mediator of sorts, and was able to pacify both combatants. It did help that both sides understood that love was the underlying motive, and that zealous emotions can make strange bedfellows.

It was during those early, mildly, stressful years that Paul's personality and true desirers emerged, then submerged, and gradually morphed. He had always wanted to be a musician; he loved classic music, and wanted to become an operatic singer. He did convince his father to allow him to take voice lessons (for pleasure he explained), but his desires were so much more; he wanted to be an operatic singer. Strangely enough, though, during this unsettling time in his life, he was aware of other passions pulling strongly at his tranquility; he began to realize that although he loved music, he also loved the uncertainties of medical challenges. Even when he was barely capable of understanding the English language, he became fascinated by the medical accounts his father would relate at the dinner table in the evening. When he didn't understand a medical term, he would, unbeknownst to his father, look up its meaning. As the months and years pasted, he amazed everyone (his father – and himself included) as to his uncanny ability to survey and diagnose a medical malady (even many that had stumped his father).

By the time Paul graduated High school, and thoughts of a higher education loomed, he had been impaled on the horns of a quandary. He loved music, but the mysteries of medical practice presented challenges he could not resist. What to do? He knew that if he chose music as a profession, he would be very happy, but there would be a void of "what if", and would be unfulfilled; and, if he chose medicine as an avocation, he would always have the loss of "what could have been as a singer".

It was during this tumultuous time that Paul de Zeus suffered an unimaginable blow, his beloved Physician Father died suddenly. It was determined that his father had perished from over work, stress, and 'caring' too much. Paul de Zeus had lost a dear friend, and mentor.

Fate had once more determined his path in life – he would go on to Medical School, and beyond. He would eventually be acknowledged by the World medical community, as a Master Diagnostician who had no peer.

Many years later, after a life-long wonderful career as a healer and diagnostician, Paul de Zeus, as he lay on his dying bed, quietly sighed –

YES, FATHER, I *DID* BECOME A DOCTOR!

PS,

But, hold on, this bitter-sweet story cannot, and will not, end without telling you – THE REST OF THE STORY.

Father de Zeus was not always a physician. In his youth, he had struggled mightily to survive during the depression years of the late twenties and thirties, and the following war years. It was during those uncertainties of life that he realized that self-determination and fortitude were required to escape the pervasive jaws of poverty that had encompassed him; his determination to become a physician would enable him to help himself – and his fellow man.

Paul de Zeus's and his siblings, Geno, Alfredo and Anita were also greatly affected by those brutal early years. Although they were annoyed by their father's constant reminder that they should become physicians, they subconsciously were pleased that someone cared enough about their lives and welfare that it enabled them to feel confident of a successful future – they didn't have to be doctors. After all, not everyone can be a doctor!

Life stories can be stranger than fiction. Alfredo, Paul's older brother, followed his own `calling`, and became a successful Geologist. The "Be a physician" pleading by his father, had sparked an inner fire that burned into his very soul, a need to learn about the elemental "stuffs" of the world around him.

Remarkably, Gino, the can do, everything, brother, followed his life's desire, the love of music; to spend a lifetime playing, and repairing musical instruments. His energies and passion for the piano knew no bounds; he spent years mastering its intricacies'; his love of music created, for him, a world of harmonious love.

So, what can be said of beautiful Anita? The call to be a doctor was not lost on her. Yes, she would surely spend a lifetime in the medical field – but not as a doctor-- she would become a nurse. She spent a lifetime of caring.

There is no doubt that the words "I don't care what you do in life, as long as you become a doctor", will resonate, in all homes where there are children, and loving and caring parents.

Who knows, there might be another

Reluctant Healer in our midst!

THE RHODODENDRON AFFAIR

Nothing in this world is more beautiful, than the flower of one of God's most magnificent creations, the rhododendron -- BUT!

Josef Rosencrantz, a renowned arbor- culturist, florist, and a lover of nature was a prominent, outspoken advocate for the protection of our natural world. He was especially vocal when he perceived harm was being done to `the loves of his life, the rhododendron flowers. He couldn't understand why all the people of the world didn't love, and appreciate the beautiful flowers of the `rose tree` -- the *rhododendron!*

Although, most people did enjoy the flower of the `rose tree`, it was, for them, just another beautiful `miracle` that mother nature had bestowed upon them to enjoy; after all, beauty is beauty -- wherever, it is found.

Strangely enough, Josef Rosencrantz's attitude about, the perceived callousness of people's indifference about the bounties of nature, seemed to change from time to time. There were times when he would become almost `manic` in his outbursts, and insisted that people should love his beloved rhododendron; and then there were times, when he appeared depressed, and uncaring; as if all flowers of the world, were meaningless.

Soon, very soon, people began to say disturbing things about him, and comments such as "the guy is looney"; if he likes the rhododendron so much, why don't we build, and lock him up, in a `rose tree!"

At first, Josef Rosencrantz didn't seem to mind the many unkind comments and remarks that were made about him. Actually, when he first heard some of the "asinine remarks, from stupid persons", he would laugh, and say ": stupid is, as stupid does". He would often be heard to say "if only people could see, and understand how beautiful the `rose tree` is; if they only knew what they're missing -- if only they knew --.

But, as the unkind remarks of strangers, AND close acquaintances, continued; he began to think DARK thoughts. He honestly didn't understand why he was being attacked, surely the reason for their venom couldn't be because he loved a magnificent flower -- no, he thought, they were attacking him for personal reasons. As time passed, his demeanor perceptibly changed, he no longer laughed and rarely spoke to anyone; he began to have headaches, and was unable to sleep. Yes, Josef Rosencrantz was near the breaking point -- something had to give!

One morning, after a horribly restless night, he awakened remarkably refreshed. He wondered how, or why, he felt so good. Ah, but now, he thought, "I can get even with all those dolts who have maligned me; "I don't want to kill them, but I sure do want them to suffer a little." During his previously restless night, he had devised a devious plan that would cause distress and pain to his tormentors, but not incriminate him;

`What a tangled web we mortals weave, when first we plan to deceive!'

Josef was a practical, knowledgeable man. He decided to implement a strategy that would create confusion, pain, and widespread fear, but, at the same time, would not have permanent or fatal consequences, in most cases; he would use the wonderful, sweet, but potentially dangerous honey that had been extracted from the -- yes, -- his beloved Rhododendron flower -- revenge is sweet -- oh, the irony of it!

As is the case, so often in life, not all matters, and things, are as sweet and cuddly, as they appear to be. It so happens that the Rhododendron and its related relative, the azalea, and other related plants, **are poisonous** (the flower, leaves et al). The poison (Grayanotoxin) is a glucoside, a compound that causes severe gastrointestinal, respiratory, cardiac arrhythmia, and sometimes death in animals and humans, by altering the calcium, sodium metabolism, at the cellular level. Josef's plan was quite simple. He would contract for large amounts of honey from the Rhododendrons fields in Turkey, and place it for sale (at almost give-away price). It was important to have honey that was not mixed with non-rhododendron honey (mixing with normal honey would dilute and negate the toxin effect). There was no doubt in his tormented mind that the large amounts of honey would quickly be bought, and eaten, by the `dolts`, and soon, would be suffering from the "Mad Honey Disease." It was a clever plan, he thought, to exact punishment, and have revenge, without being implicated. He had planned well; it was a perfect crime. His research of the "The Mad Honey Disease" had told him that `honey toxicity disease` was well known as far back as 401 BC -- it couldn't fail!

When the inexpensive honey `hit` the market, the rush was on, everybody wanted to buy as much of the honey as was allowed; it seemed that `the whole world,` loved honey. But, soon however, within six hours, the `sweet-tooth` crowd would unfortunately have a rude awakening; and the rhododendron lovers would have their revenge.

Approximately six hours after eating the wonderful honey, people began to have strange sensations and symptoms. The medical community couldn't understand, or explain, why or how, so many people would suddenly develop such unusual symptoms, in such a short period of time. There were people who were salivating and perspiring profusely; some folks were vomiting, and dizziness was commonly present; others developed low blood pressure, and lack of coordination. It seemed that the entire community had suddenly developed `the flu`. Several people were hospitalized for dehydration, and heart rhythm abnormalities, but there were no deaths. Within twenty four hours, the "flu" had run its course, and most people recovered.

It really didn't take the medical community too long to put two -and -two together, to realize that something was` rotten in Denmark,` there *had to be* a common culprit that was responsible for the widespread and sudden appearance of such mayhem. After interrogations of many of the victims, a common theme ensued; they had all eaten some honey prior to their symptoms. It didn't take long for the toxicology laboratory to identify the poison that was responsible for all their symptoms; it was, Grayanotoxin, the poison of the Rhododendron, the cause of -- `The Mad Honey Disease`.

The final question needed to be asked: "why did the honey have a toxin in it, where did it come from, and who was responsible". Unfortunately for Josef, many of the irate poison victims shouted, loud and clear, -- it was Josef, the 'rhododendron nut, ' who was responsible.

It was only a matter of checking records, and poor Josef's 'perfect crime' went - up in smoke -- and, 'the best laid plans are ---. 'Josef was then apprehended and placed in custodial care until he had his day in court. It was decided that a psychiatric evaluation of Josef's mental health be performed before trial began. His medical evaluation was sad, but somewhat expected, by many. The psychiatric opinion was as follows: Josef is an intelligent man who loves nature, and flowers, but, alas, is affected with a mental illness; he is a Manic Depressive, and is unable to overcome periods of excessive activity, or severe mental lows (depression).

It was the court's decision, that Josef should not be punished, because he was mentally ill. It was recommended that Josef remain under psychiatric care for treatment, and have periodic psychiatric evaluations.

PS,

The court's decision and the shame of being arrested were too much for Josef, he slipped into a deep depressive state, and decided to 'end it all'

One morning they found Josef dead in bed -- he had died of Grayanotoxin poisoning (he had eaten many rhododendron leaves). His friends, and some flower lovers, buried him with a rhododendron flower in his hand, and surrounded his grave site, with many rhododendron and azalea plants.

It is a fitting farewell

THE ROSE OF SHARON

If there is a love of `beauty` in your soul, then surely, you will cherish the delicate, and majestic `Rose of Sharon`; it is a flower that becomes more beautiful each time it is gazed upon. Would it be possible to live in a world that is devoid of the beauty and grandeur of a flower; would it be possible, to exist, without breathing? It is the existence of a protective loving cocoon, created by Mother Nature's miraculous bounty of flowers; the gentle stalwarts of the forests, and blessedly, her bounteous gifts of nature, that nurture and permit us to flourish contently in this, our turbulent stress-laden world.

The `rose of Sharon` is the modern name given to two lovely flowers that differ slightly in appearance, but are equal in beauty and majesty. As is often the case when creations of great beauty are present that the world's citizens have taken notice, and have revered and incorporated the essence of the flowers, in thought and deed.

Although the name `Rose of Sharon, ` as used in modern times refers to only two flowers: the Hypericum Calycinum, and Hibiscus Syriacus, there are other flowers such as the Crocus "Sharon" found in Harper's bible dictionary; the Tulipa Montana -- a bright red tulip-like flower that is found in the hills of Sharon; and the Tulipa Agenensis -- a species loved by Botanists. Although, all the flowers mentioned are beautiful and revered by many people of our world the `Rose of Sharon` IS NOT A ROSE in most Countries, but, it is possible that the "rose of Sharon" is a Cistus (a rock rose) found in Palestine, and at Mt. Carmel where especially, the Cistus abounds in April, and where it covers much of the barer parts of the mountain.

So a rose is a rose, may not be a rose but -- could be a rose!

Interestingly enough, the poet Robert Herrick (1591-1674) wrote the poem "to his Savior, a child, a present by a child" to the baby Jesus- and told him, He *is* the Rose of Sharon known. The Rose of Sharon, is a biblical name, and first appeared in 1641 in the King James Version of the bible.

The flower, *Hibiscus Syriacus*, that is known today as `*The rose of Sharon*`, appears in many yards and gardens; it is a soothing balm for our harried souls.

The flower, Hypericum Calycinum, is also known as the

And so, it seems, that the gentle, benevolent `curator of all things` (of nature, man and sea), had the great forethought to assemble, and nurture's offerings of such magnificent beauty, the Rose(s) of Sharon; they are blessings that bursts upon us in late summer and fall, with their many offerings of magnificence -- when all others, had shone --and passed away.

THE SAND DOLLAR

Several years ago, I wrote a short story "Walking along the sea shore". It was then that I remember thinking, as I encountered nature's exquisite bounties, "What a blessing it is, just to be alive in such a splendorous world; and I remember how I then innocently mused:

"Gosh, the mysteries encountered on this sandy beach are, yet, another story. You need only to look more closely to realize that this is a vast community of living creatures both on the surface of the sand, and beneath. With a little luck you might find a moon snail or a surf crab; both depend on the ever-present surging of the waves for their food; and, just below the surface of the sand, another world of living creatures can be found. The most recognized and sought after specimen, is the scaled down relative of the Sea Urchin, better known as the "Sand Dollar. Perhaps the most secretive of the underground creatures are the *ghost crabs,* or the ghost shrimp; their existence is evident by the telltale small fecal pellets found on the sand near their subterranean entrance."

The word `innocent` used earlier, was the realization of how little I knew about `sea life`, and how blandly, and `matter-of-factly` I had dismissed, a truly spectacular resident of our planet – the Sand Dollar! I suppose, one can be excused for a temporary lapse of appreciation, and acknowledgement, when the senses are overwhelmed, with brain numbing beauty, e.g., – "As I continued along the beach I viewed a breath-taking, panoramic view of offshore shrimp boats plying their trade, with myriads of sea gulls hovering above them frantically trying to wrest an unfortunate fish from one another; and then amidst the flying turmoil, an awkward appearing, but agile, pelican, was seen making a "dive bomber" attack on an unsuspecting fish below. And, yes, there were birds of all descriptions. On some areas of the beach, many pelicans were congregated; as many as 75 of these magnificent creatures were defiantly strutting, and vociferously trying to outdo each other for tiny morsels of food. On another area of the beach, large numbers of gulls stood stationary along the shore, with their backs windward, resembling exquisitely carved sand statues; as I approached, they moved in unison, only when collision was imminent. Perhaps, the most active and colorful participants on the shore were the sand pipers and sanderlings. They looked like programmed toys as they followed the retreating waves for any tiny snack; only to then quickly retreat from the oncoming waves; their movements were so precise that they resembled a well- choreographed stage play"

Yes, I had been truly mesmerized by nature's many miracles of form and design.

And, now,

THE SAND DOLLAR

But, what are sand dollars?

The sand dollar is another example of a 'creative' living sea creature; that is capable of free-swimming, as a larvae early-on, but then, after "growing up," become mostly immobile as their hard skeleton begins to form; it is at this heavier stage of development that they drop to the bottom of the ocean, and live there for the rest of their lives.

When they are alive, they are a dark color, covered with short dark spines (fur-like). The spines provide locomotion, such as it is, but more importantly, the spines catch bits of food, and then their tiny fan-like cilia propel the tiny pieces of food along 'food' groves located along its -- star-shaped Skelton, to its mouth. Its diet is varied (crustacean larvae, small copepods (small crustaceans), diatoms (algae) and detritus (particulate organic material)).

Remarkably, the sand dollar has 'tube feet' that emanate from the top of the shell; along pathways that resemble the pedals of a flower. Along each pedal (5) there are many tiny holes through which the tube feet protrude. Tube feet are not used to move around – they are used – to breathe!

Sand dollars reproduce by releasing eggs and sperm into the water, where they join and develop into free swimming larvae. After several development steps, their skeleton starts to form (and harden) – and soon thereafter -- down to the bottom they go – and become, permanent bottom dwellers. It seems that the `dollar` does very well, on the ocean floor. They move slowly, but effectively, via their tiny spines. They are able to position themselves at an angle facing the oncoming currents to catch food, or from being washed away; and, are wisely, or instinctively capable of embedding themselves under the sand for protection.

The `Story` of the SAND DOLLAR cannot, and will not, end by merely describing its life cycle, color, or whatever; there is so much more mystery to its presence. One need only to look more closely, to realize that, although the sand dollar is `just a seashell,` it commands attention, and even reverence, by many folks. If it's `dead shell` is carefully scrutinized, the beauty of its etchings, and significance of its structure, inspire awe and contentment.

Allow me the pleasure of reproducing for you, a beautiful poem that immortalizes this simple, but majestic creation – known as the "SAND DOLLAR". I do not know its author, but am grateful for its creation.

The legend of the sand dollar

Here's a lovely little story

That so many men will tell,

Of the life and death of Jesus

Etched upon this lonely shell.

If you look at it real closely,

You will find an image here

Of four nails and another

From a Roman's sharpened spear.

One side shows the Easter Lilly

With its center as a star,

That shined brightly for the Shepherds

As they traveled from afar.

And the Yuletide poinsettia

Painted on the other side

Tells us Christ was born on Christmas

Wore our cross until he died.

If you break the center open,

You will find the sign of peace

Five white doves *in gleaming beauty,*

Will its wonders never cease!

So you see the simple story;

Jesus lived for you and me.

To carry on his work on earth,

To love humanity.

THE SINGER

I have a story to tell you that will soften the tentacles of everyday stress, and will make you proud to be a human being. It is a story of a humanist (a person having a strong interest in, and concern for human welfare); yet, it is a story that is repeated so often in our daily lives, in so many ways, and by so-many caring individuals, but shamefully, their caring and thoughtfulness, is often perceived as just being a 'nice' gesture, or, it's 'OK' -- and then forgotten. Although I have titled this story "The Singer", I could have titled it "The Angel"; or "The Guitarist," or the "Mouth-organist," because the angel, I am about to tell you about, did in fact sing and intermittently play the guitar -- and -- a Mouth Organ (free weed aerophone with one or more air chambers fitted with a free reed) -- (Wikipedia). No, I don't think it was the best musical program ever performed, but the love for his audience (of physically compromised, aged, and tortured souls), exuded with every musical note -- he was truly, a star, shining brightly -- 'An Angel'.

THE SINGER

One Tuesday morning I, once again, went to the nursing home, as I do every day of the year, to help my wife with her lunch and supper; I do so, because she is suffering with Alzheimer's disease and is unable to feed herself. This Tuesday morning was no different than all the many other Tuesdays of the year, except that this time, I, for some unknown reason, had arrived at the nursing home a little earlier than usual. I am deliberately agonizing over 'my time of arrival' at the nursing home, because my having been early, meant that I was able to witness and hear the performance of a musician who was singing, and playing his instruments with loving attention, to a roomful of 'wounded, and the 'aged' (residents) of the nursing home.

As I entered the nursing home, and unexpectedly heard music, I, confused, wondered what was going on, because I had never experienced a 'musical' performance so early in the day at the nursing home. After inquiring, I was told that the singer was an amateur musician who volunteered to entertain the nursing home residents.

I soon found my wife sitting in her wheel chair in the back of the room; she appeared to be completely mesmerized by the "goings on". A wonderful elderly fellow resident sitting next to her beckoned for me to come to her, and whispered "your wife is having such a good time, she loves the music"; naturally, her telling me that, "was music to MY ears," because my wife rarely reacts to 'any stimuli' because of her Alzheimer's malady YES, this Tuesday, was destined to be a grand day for me; there aren't too many sunshine days in our 'Alzheimer's malady, world of shadows'.

Following the 'singer's performance, the audience acknowledged him with muted applause, but remained quiet for a long time; they had heard a caring, middle aged, slightly balding singer, belt out 'country-tunes' of yesteryear, that were familiar, and gently and emotionally rendered, with artistry and 'feeling'. He, after his performance, slowly sought out each and every member of the audience, who was unable to sit up or talk, and gently, squeezed an arm, or hand, and whispered 'God speed,' to them. It was at that moment, that I was certain, that the wonderful performance that I had just seen and heard was not presented by a graying, paunchy, old has-been, but was truly -- an Angel in disguise, that had come to comfort the aged and infirmed, in this, their 'hour', of tears.

Intrigued, and grateful, that I had been able to see and hear his performance, I asked several residents of the nursing home following the performance if they had enjoyed the music. They all responded with a smile, and nodded, yes. I am not only reasonably sure that they enjoyed the music, but I am absolutely sure that having an Angel come to them, even for such a short time, was, 'so very much' appreciated; **they were grateful, that somebody cared enough to come and entertained them; and that, blessedly, they had not been forgotten.**

Yes, thankfully, there are occasional groups of amateur performers that do come to the nursing home to entertain the residents. Usually, the entertainers come in the evenings, shortly after suppertime, and before bedtime, i.e. 7PM.

Some of the amateur performers are remarkably talented; some are religiously inclined; others are associated with local skilled, dance, or voice groups, and are, as our present 'Country Singer 'is, tainted with the tincture of 'milk of human kindness'.

But, talented or not, ALL who do come, are caring ANGELS who come to help those who are helpless, and are in need of support and kindness; and that hopefully, will make lives a little happier; in this place, in this cloistered world of 'tears'.

THE SWAN

Isn't it strange? Isn't it remarkable that it took me a lifetime to notice, I mean, REALLY notice, and appreciate, one of God's most remarkable, and beautiful treasures – the Swan. Yes, the swan, a white featured, yellow beaked swan. Oh, even a city fellow like me knew about, and occasionally read about swans, but in all fairness, I really wasn't "into swans", early on, in my life – what a pity!

The other day, I inattentively was looking out of our picture window while having my morning, wake-me-up coffee, when I noticed a white object that seemed to be floating on our small lake in North East, Ohio. At first, I thought it was white trash floating on the water, but soon realized the darn thing was alive and moving. I suppose the mysterious object wouldn't have been a mysterious object, if I were a little younger, and had better vision. So, with my trusty binoculars, I was gratified to see a 'vision' that silently uplifted my soul – *it was a beautiful white feathered Swan.*

I have to be honest, and tell you, that over the past 40 years, there have been many other birds, such as the swan's closely related relative, the Canada Goose, and various other species such as Mallards, and domestic white ducks that are permanent residents on the lake, but it is a rare occasion when a swan graces our little 'pond'.

Following that first sighting, it appeared that my beautiful 'vision' had moved on to more 'fertile grounds' since I could no longer locate her on the following few days. But Just about the time that I was resigned to not seeing my 'vision' again, there, just a few feet from where I stood, there, in all her glory, was my 'vision' -- my white feathered, yellow beaked, swan. I have no idea how she was able to get so close to me without being seen, but there she was (I use the gender she, but maybe, she was a he); there is no way to differentiate the gender of a swan from a distance, other than size and weight. The male swan is usually larger and heavier. The fact that she approached me so closely was startling enough, but she did so, when I was mowing a section of the lawn that was very close to the water's edge. Why the riding mower's clatter didn't frighten her, I have no idea – I guess, as I have said many times –THINGS HAPPEN!

I know that making such a fuss over a Swan is kind of quirky, especially when a person, such as myself, who is pushing 88 years of age, is kind of – well, --is kind of --- Unusual? But consider: what if one is at a stage of life, when, as Wadsworth once wrote, "The world is too much with us". So, then, when a thing of beauty does appear, wouldn't such a magnificent creation "comfort the wild beast in all of us?" Yes! Of course, --- the creation could be a swan; or perhaps a delicate pedal of a beautiful rose; or the smile of a friend --- are all created, to soften, and provide comfort to the sinews that bind us to the task of living from day to day – they are, gratefully, a balm, a salvation for our harried souls.

Now, what was I saying?

Oh, yes, the Swan.

I'm sure we all know what a swan is, and what they look like – but, do we? I guess I should have known that there are many species of Swans. They, the Swans, come in different shades and colors, but "My Swan" has white feathers' and yellow beak – it is a Mute Swan. If I were to impress you, I would have mentioned their scientific classification, and glibly noted their Kingdom, Phylum, Class, Order, Family and Genus; but, I will just say:

A SWAN, IS A SWAN – A BEAUTIFUL SWAN!

A

MUTE SWAN

But there are other species of Swans:

There are the Trumpeter; Whooper; Black necked; Tundra: and Bewick's Swans. The young swans are Swanlings, or cygnets = (little); the male is a Cob (Cobb = leader of a group), and the female is a Pen.

So, what else would one need to know?

THE TEN ARMED SWIMMER

I recently learned something new. I learned something that I thought I knew; and remarkably, it (the new something), was learned one day while having lunch. I'm sure my "new" something is probably 'old hat' for most folks, but what the heck, us old guys can't know and remember everything. One would think that someone who had managed to stay alive for 88 years would know something about SQUID; yep, it was quid that had been ordered by my host as an entrée for our lunch. When I surveyed the plate filled with the many strands of 'something' "fishy", I cried OCTOPUS! Well. I was close, but no cigar; although they are in many ways similar to the octopus, *the tangled mess on the plate -- was squid.*

My encounter with Mr. Squid at the luncheon table was somewhat less enjoyable (but good), than my subsequent research and learning about the squid's life, anatomy, and yes, of its forays in the deep blue seas of the world.

I must humbly admit that I did know a few facts about the squid, but I had always though squid = octopus, I couldn't have been more wrong; it's true that the squid and octopus are very similar, in many ways, such as the number of arms (10), excellent vision and intelligence and shape, but the difference ends there. The squid is relatively long lived; the octopus has a relatively short life span. The octopus is not a voracious killer, but is venomous; the squid is a predator, and probably wishes, that it could also be venomous.

Squid is a popular food in many countries of the world, e.g. Canada, Portugal, Japan, Italy, and many more. The word calamari is frequently used when squid is marketed, or when it is on the dinner menu. The term calamari is an Italian word for squid, which in turn is from a Greek word meaning ", "tube, reed" or "ink Pen." The body can be stuffed whole, cut into flat or round pieces; and remarkably, its arms, tentacles, and even the ink are edible. The only non-edible parts are the beak, and pen (part of its hard body tissue).

Our / my calamari meal experience was less than spectacular. The calamari were deep fried, and served with various "dips" that masked whatever other taste was present. I am reasonably sure that all the many peoples of the world who consider it a delicacy could not be wrong, so I am more than willing to give it another go; more about food, anon.

I mentioned the fact that the squid is a predator. It is well endowed physically to live up to its title of `predator`. This gladiator is equipped with eight arms that are arranged in pairs, and, also, has two tentacles that are `armed` with suctioned cups that have sharp, curved claws that can kill and shred prey into manageable pieces. In addition, they are armed with a robust, sharp beak and a mouth with a roughhewed tongue; and, as if the squid didn't have enough fire power to be a fearsome adversary, it is also equipped with high speed locomotion capabilities. *Although it has ten appendages (8 arms & 2 tentacles), and two swimming fins, most of its swimming potential is made possible by its `siphon and `high powered' water jet stream,* that makes it possible to speedily out maneuver their enemies and prey – it is truly, a modern, well equipped -- fighting machine!

Now, how good are squid on the dinner table? It appears that the culinary preparation of the squid, is the major determinant factor for many folks of the world, E.G., in Portugal, the squid are grilled whole with bell peppers and onions; or battered; or stuffed with minced meat. In Italy, Greece, Spain, Turkey, and others, squid rings are coated with batter and fried in oil, *but it is crucial to fry squid for just a short period of time, or slow cook with low temperature, to keep the flesh tender.* In northern Spain, squid is cooked in its own black ink, resulting in a black stew-like dish in which squid meat is very tender, and is accompanied by a black sauce made with onion, tomato, squid ink – and, whatever.

It appears, that attempts to popularize squid in the United States, in the 1970's, by touting squid as a good protein source found in squid cocktails, rings and chowder; but, alas, even though a panel of 70 food tasters enlisted for market research had given the squid dishes `high marks,` negative public perception persists.

Well, no matter, I have learned about, and eaten, calamari.

How good is that!

FYI,

Squid have three hearts – two branchial hearts that feed the gills, and a larger systemic heart that pumps blood around the body. The blood contains copper-rich protein hemocyanin for transporting oxygen. There are three chambers (two auricles, and one ventricle)

Squid have highly developed sense organs and advanced eyes similar to those of vertebrates (us). They exhibit relatively high intelligence, and use active communication when hunting. The majority are no more than 24 inches long, but `the giant squid` have reached 43 feet; remarkably, a larger squid specimen (colossal squid) was caught, in THE YEAR, 2007 weighing 1,091 pounds and measured 33 feet around.

THE WORLD ABOUNDS WITH MIRACLES
OF FORM AND SHAPE!

THE WORLD OF YESTERYEAR

When I mentioned to my young friend that the world was a better place, and a better time to be alive—"way back when," a look of "oh, my God", do I have to listen to that old foggy telling me again about how he walked twenty miles in the snow going to school "when I was young"? My response, was feigning deep thought when I witnessed the bewildered look on his face. Well, I said, maybe it was only nineteen miles to the school, and then I remarked with a sigh, sometimes it did rain kind of hard too. I then, with a "knowing" smile, told him "the rest of the story".

It really doesn't hurt to exaggerate a little bit, now and then, – does it? No matter. I will continue!

`My` rest of the story began, as I said, "way back when." But to be more precise, I arrived on this Planet during the late nineteen twenties, the second decade of the 20th century. Yes, it was in 1927 that my inauspicious odyssey began. I suppose it would have been nice if my arrival had been announced in the local newspaper --- but, alas, it wasn't! Well then, my arrival could also have been announced on television, or computer --- but there weren't any such "outlandish" digital devices then. In the year, 1927, one had to actually go to a movie theater to see a movie, since DVD's were reserved for the future generations. Ah, but it was a magnificent treat to join the happy throngs at the "movies," to see Al Jolson in The Jazz Singer (did I mention that the popcorn was superb?). Saturdays were especially wonderful because you could spend the entire afternoon watching Tom Mix and other "cowboy" movies. Sure, they were expensive (five cents) but, what the heck, you only live once!

The summers, during the "roaring twenties," and early thirties weren't all that different than the summers in the twenty first century (2015), but they were so different for me. Each summer day was special. Playtime began with first daylight, and ended when the street lights came on. It was rubber-gun fights, kick the can, and swimming in the "mud hole" by the railroad tracks (honest, there really was a mud hole). It was only later, as I got older, that reality struck'; I had to work if I wanted spending money for the expensive movies and the big bag of popcorn. Oh, well, delivering the newspapers (paper route) wasn't all that bad, and it did pay well (a penny a copy). Some weeks I made six dollars, if all the customers paid their bill.

The wintertime was especially cherished; oh, I know, it was cold, but it sure was fun-time for the kids. Winter was a time for ice skating (it didn't cost anything because ponds and backyard standing- water would freeze over). We used curtain rods for ski's, and clamp-on ices skates for the fierce hockey games. The ice skates were not too good for skating, but the two-runner blades made running "a piece-of-cake". Making a "buck" in the winter wasn't all that tough; all that was needed was a shovel, a strong back, and a driveway or sidewalk with lots of snow. We could easily make five cents to "shovel" a sidewalk, and 10 cents for a driveway. Yep, those were the "good-old-days"!

In 1927, after my arrival, great changes were heralded in aviation; Charles Lindbergh made the first solo non-stop trans-Atlantic flight from New York to Paris in a single-engine monoplane, the Spirit of St. Louis. In 1927 the Mechanical Cotton Picker was invented; and Egypt officially became independent from the British Empire. But, sadly, all was not perfect in 1927. Prohibition of alcohol was still in effect (1919-1933), and the "Twenties" ended with the Wall Street crash that devastated the financial lives of so many.

Even the scientific world added to "My" decade, of the twenties, when Arthur Compton (1892-1962) was given the Nobel Prize in physics for his discovery of the "effect" named after him – "The Compton Effect" i.e. the inelastic scattering of photons in matter results in a decrease in energy (increase in wavelength) of an X-ray, or gamma ray photon. His discovery was terribly important for science. Ah, but life goes on!

I suppose the 1920s would have been special, even if I hadn't arrived! The 1920s were the roaring, golden jazz years; communism began prospering, and the Soviet Union was born; and worst of all, the Ku Klux saw growth and acceptance.

Well, now that I have waxed poetic, what now? What has become of the birthday-boy of the 20s? Did he become the President of a nation, or a leader in industry? Did he invent, or develop some gadget to improve mankind? The answer, of course, is a simple --- Heck NO. But, it seems to me that the questions asked of me were pretentious and foolish. How many mechanical cotton pickers could have been invented? Would it not be better to ask us/me (humanity), "Did you enjoy life to the fullest? "Did you fulfill your obligations to your family, and did you add sunshine, and give warmth to your fellow man"? If the query can be answered in the affirmative, you deserve the following greeting on your special day – *of any birth year:*

Happy birthday ---- We are SO glad you are here!

THINGS HAPPEN

There is one certainty that we (all) should expect in our lifetime --- things do happen! Could you visualize a life, or world, that did not have `things` happen? I'm not sure why I thought about this subject at this time, because I have always expected `things to happen`; actually, without `things` happening, we would have to be "in another world" --- of nothingness -- you KNOW what I mean --. Yet, not too long ago, I heard a young lady (aged 90) complain bitterly, who was shouting "It's always something, it's always something". I remember thinking when I heard those words, she's right, THERE IS, always `something`. I initially agreed with her, but since I am younger than her (I am only 89), I thought she was probably too old to realize that without `things` happening, she wouldn't have to worry, about -- anything --in this world!

The real problem with it's always something question ` IS WHAT, that `something` is? Well, since it is inevitable that we, all, will have `things` happen, wouldn't it be wonderful to have all `good things` happen all the time? But alas, think for a moment, if we experience only good things in life, we would die of boredom; I mean, where is the challenge of the chase, and the fun of winning. Believe or not, we, as a human race, thrive on adversity, and problem solving. Think not? One needs only to look at the daily newspaper to see the continuing problems and adversity facing us on a daily basis -- I rest my case.

Things do happen. What specifically, are the things that happen; the answer is obvious -- ANYTHING! It would appear that sometimes `things` happen, not just because they happened, but because, according to Leonardo da Vinci (1452), quote; "It had long since come to my attention that people of accomplishment rarely sat back and let things happen to them. They went out, and happened, to things".

I, too, have long felt that we are controlled by our destiny, i.e. `things` will happen both bad, and good at times, in all of our lives. I'm sure that there are many people who will disagree with me, but Paul Auster (Author), commented in agreement; quote, "The world is so unpredictable. Things happen suddenly, unexpectedly. We want to feel we are in control of our own existence. In some ways we are, in some ways we're not. We are ruled by the forces of chance and coincidence".

So, what are we to do, when 'things' happen? Do we accept all eventualities (things) without comment, or do we put up a fight and reject whatever we don't want; and accept without a murmur, with what we agree with? It would seem to me that accepting or rejecting 'things' would both be acceptable responses depending on their importance, but with the caveat, don't waste your entire strength fighting one problem --- at the expense of ignoring other more serious and pressing situations.

Well, what else can be said about 'Things' that happen? Let me tell you what other folks, who are much wiser than I, have said.

James E. Faust (Prominent Religious Leader) said: "All of us suffer some injuries from experiences that seem to have no rhyme or reason. We cannot understand or explain them. We may never know why some things happen in this life. The reason for some of our suffering is known only to the Lord".

And finally, It appears that we, all, must accept the fact that, whether, or not we like it, 'things' are always going to happen; so I guess the prudent thing to do, is prepare yourself for 'whatever comes', and take on 'all comers' with fortitude and 'common sense, ' and do what Pierre Teilhard de Chardin (French Philosopher and Jesuit Priest) had written:

"In the final analysis, the questions of why bad things happen to good people transmutes itself into some very different questions, no longer asking why something happened, but asking how we will respond, what we intend to do now that it happened".

Ah, yes,

Amen

THINKING MAKES IT SO

Thinking makes it so. Really? What did I just say? Did I just say that if I thought that that car over there was a boat, then, that car IS a boat? Yep, that's what I said, but did I really mean that – and, is it therefore, so? No, of course not, but I sure *thought* it would be super, *if* it were a boat. But, alas, it was just a *fanciful* -- thought! Although it is true that thinking about something is really an act of producing a thought, and then, forming an opinion (a judgment) – but, as seen, thinking, doesn't *always* make it so.

Horrors, where would we be, if we were not able to think and form thoughts that *intelligently* enable us to cope with the constantly changing uncertainties of life? It is only possible to form judgments, and opinions, if, we are able to think, and rationalize; *ah, yes, thinking, does, make it so!*

The problem with 'thinking', is, we oft'time don't think. How many times have you been guilty of, or heard the phrase, "gosh, I just didn't think about that." Yep, it happens to all of us; I wonder why that is?

Some folks are heard to say "thinking wears me out" when they are confronted by an extra-ordinary stressful problem. But, *does* thinking cause fatigue, or is it possible that the 'thought, ' produced by the thinking, wore them out?

We, all the human species, and most other animal species of the world, are equipped with an organ named, 'cerebrum' (brain) that enables us to think, and do other marvelous things. The cerebrum is divided into four lobes (areas) that have different functions. Remarkably, the cerebrum is divided into two hemispheres; the right governs the creativity function, and the left is responsible for thinking logically.

The frontal lobes (areas), right and left, are responsible for WHAT and, WHO we are. OUR personalities ARE the frontal lobes; and, also, where emotions, problem solving, planning, and reasoning are managed. The frontal lobes are linked to sensory and memories centers throughout the brain, and thus, we are able to think things through, and utilize information located elsewhere in the brain. **It would be impossible to have higher-level thinking without the frontal lobes**; it is this portion of the brain that allows us to make judgments, make choices, solve problems, take action, and make future plans – and, enables us to cope with the world (the wilderness) that surrounds us. Remarkably, it is possible to be ʻintelligent, ʻ but without functioning frontal lobes, we would be a ship without a rudder, and would be unable to use that intelligence.

Although it is true that an inanimate ʻbeing' (the computer) has many of the brain's functions, such as problem solving, and other tedious tasks, and does so in a superior fashion, it cannot mimic, replace, or best the human brain, because -- it cannot cry, laugh, or feel joy – it is not capable of emotion.

Finally, the brain needs exercise, similar to the needs of a healthy muscle. The aphorism "use it, or lose it" has never been truer. Recent research has documented that new brain cells are being made throughout our lives, and that hopefully, new brain cells could replace diseased and broken cells of various diseases. So, yes, the brain's pathways, and cells can be influenced – just by the ʻthinking' -- ʻthinking – does, make it so'.

PS

Education (schooling, learning) has long been known to improve one's life, in so many ways. The benefits are derived, not necessarily from leaning new facts and figures, but from the training – of the thinking.

THINKING MAKES IT SO

TREASURES OF A NURSING HOME

Many months ago, I wrote a heart-wrenching story titled 'many goodbyes'. It is a story about placing a loved one in a nursing home for the rest of her life; it is a story about the ravages of Alzheimer's disease, and the dismemberment of a family's happiness's; it is a story of seeing a loved one on a daily basis, and nightly saying goodbye, but being unsure, and fearful, that she will not be the same person that will greet me in the morning.

Now, after many, many months of nightly goodbyes, and seeing her in the mornings, the pain of our/my loss, persists; but my daily visits, and thus, knowing better the caring personnel, and the other patients, the acuteness of my despair has ameliorated somewhat. So, hopefully, now, I am better able to help her, and others, to better cope with the despair that is so pervasive throughout the nursing home.

Shortly after arriving at the nursing home, it soon became apparent, that all was not well with many of the residents. It was obvious that apathy was prevalent, and that the behavior and activity of many of the residents seemed to be, in a state of suspended animation. Of course, it is understandable, that illness, age, and debilitation is a disheartenment cause of their 'slowness', but there seemed to be more to it than that. It soon became obvious that boredom, and lack of person to person contact was a major contributing cause of the listlessness that was so pervasively encountered.

It was during lunch and dinnertime that the various patients, at times, demonstrated their great need for friendship, and for social contact. We soon noticed that several patients would arrive at our dinner table to say hello, or mumble greetings, or, would maneuver their wheelchairs so close to our dinner table that helping my wife with her meals became difficult, or almost impossible. It was only after considerable frustration, and help from the dining room staff, that order was restored; but, it was the beginning of my subsequent odyssey into finding, and exposing, the hidden treasures that were so well camouflaged in the persons that surrounded me

As the months rolled by, I met, and learned that Lennard (I use fictitious names) had a family that he was so proud of, and when he falteringly told me of his past life, it was obvious (by the glint in his eyes) that he relished the moment that somebody cared, and would take the time to listen to him; little did he know that during our short time together, my heart cried out in joy for him.

When I met Ann (I don't know her last name) she, like many of us, had a difficult time remembering things, and was prone to repeat, repeat, and repeat. I'm sure I will remember that her husband had been a board member, and that they did travel extensively before her husband died. It was a joy to see 'that light in her eyes' as she related her story. She appeared elated, *each time* she told me her life's story -- yes, somebody did care, and took the time to listen to her; little did she know that I shared her elation.

Joseph. Is an elderly gentleman who had suffered a stroke, and is permanently bed ridden. He is transported daily to the dining room for his meals, but appears to be somnolent most of the time, and rarely smiles -- he, of course, had no reason to smile. At first, when I passed him in the hallway, I smiled a hello to him, and proceeded on my way. As time passed, I smiled and would say to him "HI, how are you doing," as I passed him; then, a few days later, I stopped briefly by the side of his gurney, and smilingly asked him, 'How's it going" and, at the same time, gently touch his arm. One day later, as I passed him, I again briefly stopped, touched his arm, and asked him "How's it going"? It was at that moment, that I knew I had penetrated his wall of pain and despair he, for the first time, managed a faint smile and nodded his head in acknowledgement. I, to this day smile, and feel strangely euphoric when I see him, because I know he is now aware of the fact that he is not alone -- he now has a friend.

Eventually, and as the days and months pasted, more and more lonely soles became friends with us. When possible, I would tell them stories about past happy events, and even mild mystery stories (if I had not forgotten -- the, who did it)! It was a joy to see them smile, and to see the glint in their eyes as they, for the moment, were with friends, and not alone in the world. So, yes indeed,

I did find great treasures in the nursing home;

And gathered them up -- from the smiles on their faces;

And, the sparkle of their eyes.

WE ALL HAVE DREAMS

I wonder how it is, that, for however the many reasons, we are able to "revert" (when things become psychologically too bewildering or frustrating for us, we may revert our thoughts, and "lives", to another happier and more satisfying time). Some folks would simply say "live in the world of dreams". Of course, we, all, have at one time or other, lived, `in the world of dreams`; it is truly an invaluable gift bequeathed to us at birth to safe-guard our minds when under duress; and thus ameliorate pain, and relieve `worldly imposition` when, as William Wordsworth, the poet, once wrote, "The world is too much with us!"

Wouldn't it be wonderful if we could simply flip a switch in our `inner being`, and `voila` we would once again be in our `happy world`? Although we aren't able to suddenly "fly" physically to another land, or to a place of happiness, we do have the capability to "fly" to any "happy land" (real, or imaginary) – just for the thinking; it is an ability known as DREAM – *we all have dreams!*

It is true that we DO all have `dreams` during some point in our lives, and it is certainly true that dreams, at times, are without substance, but there is no doubt that dreams may, at times, derive their strength and vitality from the very fabric of our birth DNA. Every living creature is endowed with their very own unique, hereditary mixture (smoldering embers) from which their dreams of life emanate.

How so? How could dreams possibly be associated (derived) from a source so distant and ethereal, as our DNA? Yes, it is the nature of our being that we are, from whence we came! One needs look no farther than one's parents, or siblings to know that our source DNA IS responsible for whom we are, and – how we dream.

There is no question that most of us will, or should, step back at one time or another, to assess our lives as unique creatures on this earth. It was at such a time that I, a fading star, reminisced idly and frightfully about my 'less than blazing trajectory' across the skies of my past life's allotted *musical* pathways, and realized how important, indeed, was "from whence I came – my DNA" When my father immigrated to this new land, he brought with him few financial possessions, but he did bring an indomitable spirit, *his beloved violin, and the love of music.* His progeny (my brother, sister, and your author, all inherited his 'smoldering musical embers' that has so enriched our lives (our world of dreams), and the lives, and dreams of our progeny

There is no doubt in my mind that the love of music had, and will always, play a dominant role in my life. Early on, very early on in my life, the love of music (especially classic music) consumed much of my life's energies. Yes, my goal in life (pre-teens -teens) was to be an operatic singer. Even though it was during the great depression, I prevailed on my father to spend five dollars of our family's meager funds to pay for my weekly voice lessons – for nine years – such was my passion! During those early years I sang in many choirs and programs. When a symphony or opera came to town, I *found* a way (with or without coin) to gain admittance – music was my life.

Serendipity then played a major role in my life, and my future endeavors. It was in 1944, and World War 2 was in full force so, I, at the tender age of 17, enlisted into the Navy to engage in the awful fray that had enveloped the world. Although I wanted to be in the submarine service I, and many other young men, were deemed better suited, and were needed, to be naval medical Corpsmen at that critical time of the war. My first tour of duty was St Abans Hospital, Long Island, NY. Although I didn't "hate" medical 'stuff', music was still in my every thought. It was then, during my medical tour of duty at Long Island, New York, that a near fatal blow to my emotional well-being was dealt. It was in early 1945 that I consulted Music (voice) Professional, in New York City, to evaluate my voice, and determine my future voice training. Tragically, unexpectedly, I was told that my voice, and abilities, were "good enough", but I would never be "Great". The words "good enough, and never" tore through my very soul at that moment, and for days thereafter, I was a lost sailor, on a turbulent sea; I had lost my will to continue – I had lost, emotionally, the only friend I thought I could trust – my voice.

It was in early 1945, when I, and two other Medical corpsmen, was transferred to a naval base in Brunswick Maine, to staff a small medical clinic. It was our responsibility to standby and to assist in medical emergencies, if needed, when airplanes landed and took off; and, in addition, to conduct a general medical clinic.

The subsequent months at the airfield were stressful, but fulfilling for me. I felt needed and, once again, began to have happy thoughts. I loved the medical work and its challenges; **an epiphany had occurred** – I knew then, God willing, that my future work in life would be in the medical sciences; and I would become a Medical Doctor! I gradually began to realize that it's possible to love various things in life, but that music would continue to be the balm and savior of my soul. I finally was comforted, and knew then what would be my direction in life, if I should survive the war.

Yes, I did become a Doctor of Medicine in 1954, and happily provided medical care as an Internal Medicine Physician, for well over 30 years; and yes, the sound of music is still firmly ensconced, with love, in my heart.

Yes, we all have dreams

We all MUST have dreams!

We all, MUST, have a dream to follow.

WELCOME

Have you ever witnessed something that truly amazed you, and then, without thinking, said, "How in the world?" I'll bet, during these past many years, I've uttered "How in the world," thousands of times. Why in the world would I do that, I wonder? I suppose we all encounter `things` in our daily lives that startle us, or, we witness `something that is beyond the pale` (over the top) that elicits an involuntary reaction, and we utter words expressing Incredulity.

-- Words such as "how in the world", or, "holy smokes"! Well, the other day I researched the dictionary for the meaning of the word, `Welcome`. I have no idea why I needed to look up the word, because I, and everybody else, knows that the word means --, er, ah, humnn – YOU'RE WELCOME? I was astounded; I simply could not find a suitable meaning, for the word – welcome; but, honestly, I know what it means --, or do I?

After consulting the dictionary, I uttered– "holly smoke" – really! I had always depended on the word-wise wisdom of the dictionary, but now, after reading the dictionary's meaning of the word `welcome`, I'm not so sure! I have to tell you that I was truly amazed, as I reviewed the synonyms attributed to the word, welcome. I suppose we all should know that: -- comfortable; wanted; comfy; relaxed; at home, and at ease; well, according to the dictionary, they *are all interchangeable* words for the word, welcome—honest -- Holly smokes!

But really, what does the word, welcome, mean? Ah, I know! The word, welcome, is a short word, but it is full of meaning. For instance: If a guest is welcome to a home, party, or at work, he/ she are received with pleasure and with hospitality by the host. Of course, if the guests were *not* wanted, they would receive an *unfriendly* welcome (reception), and advised to not overstay their --- welcome!

So, I guess the dictionary is correct; if you approach their synonyms in the proper way, i.e. if I invited someone I liked to my home, it would make me happy, and I would be – *comfortable*, because that 'someone,' was –*wanted*.

Ah yes, now it's perfectly clear what the word welcome means; it means er, humnn, ah oh. Of course, if I say you are welcome – I mean:

Hi – I'm sure glad you're here.

What goes around, comes around

Several years ago, I had written a short story titled "THE MIRROW OF TIME LONG PAST". At that time period of my life (at aged 74 -- 14 years ago), I briefly reviewed the shortcomings and goings of my own 'personal little world'; and reflected on some of my thoughts about life's challenges and responsibilities. I then asked myself the question "I wonder how many of us would have the courage, or for that matter, the need to look back over time, for the express purpose of self-evaluation, and mused, "What would be the purpose of self-flagellation"? I then answered "well, I suppose there would be no real reason, other than it would be like an artist stepping back to evaluate his latest painting". I then innocently remarked "There is no doubt that most of us will, or should, step back at one time or another, to assess our lives as unique creatures on this earth".

So, I guess, my original summation of 'Man's' emotional need for self- gratification and self-flagellation (self-whipping) are inevitable truths, because I now have a personal dilemma that I will share with whoever will listen, and hopefully, my confession might help others. It is an honest error that I didn't realize existed, until recently (now that I am an old man, of 89 years).

My secret is really a story of life's living realities; it is a bittersweet saga of having lived a lifetime thinking that I had fulfilled my obligations and duties as a husband and father, only to realize later, much later, that I had made honest mistakes of 'inattention,' and consequently, failed to realize the significance, and harm, that may have, or could have, possibly resulted.

Many years ago, I, a young man, was happily married, had children, and was immersed in a very active medical practice. It was during that period of time when I was so very busy, and occupied with my medical duties, that I innocently and ignorantly failed to understand the emotional needs of my family; but in truth, I honestly never, even remotely, thought that I wasn't "a good father or husband." I dearly loved all my family and would have given my life for them if needed. We, as a family, did many things together; we were, I thought, a happy family.

But, it wasn't until many years later (my senior year, at age, 89) that I looked into the 'mirror of time long past' to re-evaluate my life's journey; it was then, at that time, that I realized my many past mistakes; and hence, sadly, must now administer mental self-flagellation.

Yes, what goes around DOES come around.

My story

Who would have thought that three words "Daddy, let's talk," spoken by a 5 year-old child during the depression years, would be the nidus (the origin) of my regret -- let me explain ---

The times were difficult during the depression years, and most folks, during those brutal times were 'hard pressed' to earn enough to feed their families -- and so it was with our family, in 1932, when I was 5 years old. Perhaps, my family's problems were more devastating than most, because our mother died when I was only one year old, and left four children with a father who, desperately worked, day and night to make ends meet; he never remarried. Although he loved his children, he had precious little time to give them the love and attention that was so much needed by the children.

It was, when I was 5 years old, that one day, when my father was home (he worked until 1 am, and returned to work at 7 am, every day), I mustered the courage to say to my father "Daddy, let's talk," and then asked him, "will you wake me up when you come home tonight so I can talk to you"? Yes, he did wake me up the next morning (2 am) when he got home from work, and we talked and talked, and talked. I have no idea what we talked about -- but it was so terribly important to me that I was able **to BE with** my father. It was a wonderful moment in time for me; he even brought me two "hot dogs" covered with a Greek sauce that he knew I loved. So there I was, sitting up in bed, eating hot dogs covered with a wonderful Greek sauce, at 2 o'clock in the morning, with a loving father who listened to his 5 year old son; a son who was talking non-stop -- about nothing -- and everything. It just couldn't get any better than that, for this 5 year old.

Fast forward

It is now 31 years later, and the young lad of 5, is now the father of a 5 year old daughter; a daughter, who he loves very much. Although (our five-year old lad of yesteryear) tried to be a good father to all of his children, he in 1963, was hopelessly mired in making a living, and was emotionally and physically involved in his new profession as a medical doctor. He, without realizing, had apparently, not attended to the emotional needs of his family because, yes, the inevitable happened -- **what goes around, does come around**; his precious five year old daughter came to him one day and said "Daddy, let's talk." **Remarkably, I, even then, did not understand that her request to talk was so much deeper than the need to 'talk' with her father; IT WAS HER NEED FOR THE LOVE, AND PRESENCE of her father; just as it was, for the five year old lad, in 1932.**

I suppose we could belatedly explain the reasons why we do, or don't do something in our lives, but would it alter the reality?

Perhaps this confession of my shortcomings' will alert others to the realization that providing sustenance for survival is surely important, but providing for the emotional, and mental needs, are critical requirements -- for the stability, wholeness, and happiness -- of us all.

There certainly are circumstances in life that are uncontrollable. But, would it not be helpful if we could understand all the aspects 'of that circumstance', and then correct, or prevent such hurtful outcomes, as mine?

Unhappily, I must admit, that the aphorism:

Olt too soon, schmart too late;

Is, -- SO very true.

WHEN DID IT ALL START?

I suppose I should begin this beginning, by asking the question "When will it all end -- for me?" Today was one of those days that posited more questions than answers; it is also the day that upon wakening in the morning, I realized that I was one year older, and knew, `time` was the great equalizer of all human endeavors -- and yes, `time` ALWAYS has the last say! Yep, I had just joined the eighty nine-year old club of old f--ts! But what has all this to do with -- `When did it all start`?

For the past several years, I had innocently jotted down little reminders about some of my `finer` moments (of good stuff) in my life, so that `later on`, I would, just maybe, write a book -- or `something` (doesn't everyone do that?). Actually, I never, ever, thought that I would, or could, write a book; but what the heck, it did make me feel just a little bit `important` thinking about it (someone once had told me that it was easy to `write a book`; all I had to do was to just start writing).

But, when did it ("I" start) -- to write?

Actually, it was during my first encounter with English Composition during my first year in college, that I was sort of fascinated with putting `words together` so that they would say something meaningful. I had no ideas about being an AUTHOR then, -- nor do I now, but it has always been fun for me to `write`. I not only wrote my own little required college compositions, but I also wrote a few `assignment papers` for my two brothers, when they were struggling through `English composition 101`. But, as we all know, writing a `Pulitzer` is not a first priority for most students as they proceed, struggling, ever higher in the academic world -- there is simply too much `stuff` to hurriedly record, and make legible, the lecture material to be memorized later; so, we used all kinds of shortcuts, slashes, and abbreviations to produce our notes -- and pray, we would be able to decipher them later -- Pulitzer-- be darned! Somehow, or other, I managed to pass my English composition courses, only to be confronted later on, by the `real world` i.e., the world of harsh critics -- the `reading world`. But, not to be deterred, I delved fearlessly into the world of prose when I encountered an interesting life experience.

Soon, after opening my office to Practice Medicine in the late 1950's, I encountered many, many `interesting life experiences, but I had become so occupied with my `world of stress` that `writing` was the last thing on my mind -- I had enough on my plate with the problems on hand, that writing, would have to wait `for another day`.

Destiny (fate) is often the mediator of one's course in life; and so it was for me; when my only daughter was struck down by a calamitous medical mishap my life was changed forever. It was at that moment, that I, in deep despair, wrote, `In Memory of a Duck` and dedicated it to my own lost little duck. It is a true story, of the lives and loves of two white ducks, and a gallant Canada goose. It was after the untimely, traumatic death of one of the white ducks, that I witnessed a scene of such tenderness, and poignant beauty, that I wrote at the terminus of my story `IN MEMORY OF A DUCK`: -- "Following the attack, I looked down from the road to their open area near the water's edge, and sadly witnessed a heartbreaking scene. There, stood a goose, silently, gently, scratching at a few remaining white feathers of his lost friend". I was vividly reminded that the loss of a loved one is a universally painful event -- for all creatures large, or small.

During the following days and months, I, in deep despair from the loss of my own little duck, felt the compelling need to `write something`, it really didn't matter that I couldn't type, or comprehend the value of a computer, so I scribbled senselessly on countless sheets of paper. I then, foolishly, sent my poorly written `notes` to a typist who tried to decipher my scribbles into readable print -- but, alas, for a sizable fee. It didn't take me too long to realize that I HAD to learn to type, and get a computer. So, as we all know, `thinking makes it so`; hence, my age be darned, I eventually reached an acceptable two-finger `typing expertise`, and was soon able to eliminate the `middleman`; I was now a freelance author!

The following few years were rewarding for me because I continued to write short stories about subjects that interested me, and remarkably, some people actually read them; and, even more amazingly, commented that they liked them. I had never considered the prospect of benefitting financially, or to have my stories published -- it was reward enough that I had retained my sanity, by writing, and thus, had somewhat ameliorated the ever-present pain of the loss of my loved one.

Sometimes, it seems that misfortune has a life of its own, because a few years later, my wife was struck-down by Alzheimer's disease that eventually necessitated permanent Nursing home care. It was at that time of our lives that I turned my attention, and my writings, to the horrors of Alzheimer's disease. I had determined that perhaps, just perhaps, I could, in some way, write stories that would call attention to, and possibly accelerate medical research that would prevent, cure, or reasonably treat, this malevolent scourge that destroys all who are afflicted, or exposed, to its deadly venomous tentacles.

Now, the rest of the story

One day, while I was helping my wife with her lunch, a group of quality assurance examiners from the state, had arrived for their yearly visit at the nursing home. Shortly after they had arrived, one of the examiners approached our table, and asked if I would comment on the care my wife was receiving. I, of course, told her that the quality of care was excellent. She then asked me the reason my wife had to be in a nursing home. I then explained to her that I had cared for her at home for five years, until my advanced age, and the complications of her Alzheimer's malady, made it too difficult for me to continue her care at home. I told her that I had recently written a short story chronicling her descent into the 'World of Shadows'. It was at that moment, when she heard what I had said, softly whispered, with tears in her eyes, "my father just recently died from that horrible disease; please let me read your story."

After she had read my story 'DESCENDING INTO THE WORLD OF SHADOWS', she begged me to have my stories published, so that others who are suffering from that horrible plague might be helped.

And so, after many letters from that wonderful 'agent of destiny', her mother, and many others, I decided to have my stories published (even if they weren't 'Pulitzer' quality). An **epiphany** had occurred for me (an experience of sudden and striking realization); I knew, then, what I had to do.

Hopefully, my efforts will help in some small way to eliminate this Alzheimer's scourge that has enveloped so many millions of souls in its deadly tentacles.

Surely, *there is room for one more miracle!*

PS,

At the onset of this feckless discussion, I had asked "what does my age have to do with -- anything?" Well, nothing I suppose except that I fear, that I will not be able to fulfill my pledge to protect, and accompany my wounded angel until she once again, will be able fly forever, in a world of happiness.

WHEN THE SUN GOES DOWN

It comes as no surprise to me that diseases sometimes exercise their diabolic schemas in the shade of darkness; and so it is, with `THE DISEASE OF DARKNESS `the malady known as Alzheimer's Disease. There is no doubt, that as the victims of this dreaded malady slip silently, slowly, into the World of Shadows, they manifest their anger, anxiety, fear and anguish, by striking out in retaliation; they have no other way available for them to plead for help, or to express their horror of being dehumanized with the slow loss of their mind and body treasures. So, yes, they do strike out at whoever is near, with violence (at times), exhibit anger, hide things, and exhibit anguish with uncontrolled crying. Their emotions are so confused and tormented that, without rhyme or reason, may explode into severe moments of agitation, pacing, stubbornness, rocking, hitting -- and -- wandering. Sadly, alas, the term Sundowner Syndrome has become synonymous with the wild uninhibited behavior of the Alzheimer's victim, and seems to commence more aggressively, `when the sun goes down`.

Although there are various reasons postulated for the seemingly altered demeanor of the tormented Alzheimer afflicted person when the `sun goes down`, but there really is no true scientific explanation. For example, some Medical Experts believe that the Sundown Syndrome is caused by the overwhelming accumulation of daily stress that erupts at twilight. Other opinions are: simple stress buildup; hormonal imbalance; and some believe the pending darkness causes anxiety because the victims fear of not being able to see, or have fear `of getting lost`.

There is no doubt that all of the above theories are possible, and could possibly explain the Sundown Syndrome, when analyzed singly or in combination; but permit me to offer my thoughts on the matter.

Firstly, some background, upon which my observations, thoughts, and opinions are based.

Unfortunately, destiny (fate) had inflicted my loving wife of 64 years with this mysterious malady, Alzheimer's disease, when she was 78 years old; I have previously written a short story titled 'Descending into the world of shadows,' describing her descent into, 'her world of tears'. I, her husband, a retired Physician of Internal Medicine, have lived with, loved and cared for her, on a daily basis for these past nine years of her disease, and have witnessed helplessly, with horror, her torment.

A PARAGRAPH, from my 'Descending into the world of shadows' story:

"When her illness first appeared, her symptomatology (her symptom complex) varied as her disease progressed. Initially, she had an occasional memory lapse that caused her slight embarrassment, but she shrugged it off with the comment "oh, it wasn't important anyway". As the weeks and months passed, other symptoms appeared that were not appreciated by her, but were obvious to others. It became apparent that her personality would change (combative, restless, agitated) as evenings approached, around 5-6 PM – the so-called "sundown syndrome"). After a few more months, her agitation began to appear earlier and earlier. Today, a simple word at any time, or an innocent comment by me, or others, will cause her to strike out, and resist attempts to mollify her"

As is often the case, one disease process, will often lead to other disabilities. When she had developed pneumonia and required hospitalization, she rapidly became more combative, and physically incapable, so that she required more intensive care of a Nursing Home following her hospitalization.

It was while she was in the nursing home that I had resolved to try and help her overcome the hurtful sundowner symptoms that were roiling within her.

For the past four years, I have been with her on a daily basis, for her lunch, and supper meals at the nursing home. Initially, her meal times -- were her combat times, and to say the least, it was a very 'stressful time' for me. It was during those turbulent mealtimes, that I decided on a 'game plan' to help her fight her internal demons. I remembered, that during our very happy marriage of 64 years, that my dear wife would fall asleep whenever I would read a story or sing to her; and, I also remembered the 'saying' "music soothes the wild beast in all of us"; SO, I decided to begin talking to her about our past happy memories, and sing to her, prior to meal time. Of course, I realized that she may not understand what I was saying or that she wouldn't appreciate my singing; but, it was the best I could do, and strangely, it made me feel better. During the first few weeks of my experiment, there were many mishaps i.e. cups and dishes etc. were thrown on the floor, and many outbursts of aggressive behavior. Initially, when I sang to her, she would deliberately 'look all around the room', and never look at me. Nevertheless, I continued to sing my love song "YOU ARE MY SUNSHINE" to her. Then, one day, as I was singing **our love song,** she actually began to 'act nice' and appeared to 'like' my singing; she even smiled a little. It was at that moment, that I knew I had penetrated the barriers of her internal demon -- and had exorcised him -- hopefully, forever. *Today, she actually 'loves' to hear HER/ MY love song 'you are my Sunshine' and, her mealtimes, are mostly happy affairs since her 'Sundowner Demon' has been tamed.*

There is no doubt in my mind, that love and caring (tempered with patience, and a little music), are powerful allies when fighting the malevolent forces observed in Alzheimer's disease. I also believe that the depth and degree of the Sundown Syndrome outbursts are partially determined by the victim's pre-illness personality (DNA). That is to say, if the victim's personality is strong-willed, and assertive, might not the sundown syndrome reflect those attributes, *in an unconstrained manner?*

PS,

I would now like to tell you about some other observations, and thoughts, concerning the Alzheimer's syndrome that I have garnered over the past four years of close attendance to my wife's needs.

I suppose, it should go without saying, that the most important aspect of any medical treatment --- is having the correct diagnosis. When a person is thought to have Alzheimer's disease, an extensive, thorough medical examination --- **is mandatory**. It is never permissible to assume, or guess; you could be DEAD wrong!

It is well known, that there are many medical conditions that mimic or resemble Alzheimer's disease; i.e. disorders such as brain tumors, or brain involvement such as hematoma, normal pressure hydrocephalus (increased pressure on the brain), brain injury; and many other medical conditions such as Vitamin B-12 and thyroid deficiencies, depressive states, infection, and substance abuse.

In recent times, I am personally aware of two instances of Alzheimer patients dying, **with a previously undiagnosed** brain tumor. You might glibly say "So what, all is lost with brain tumors, anyway". Ah, but not so fast, it has recently been documented that, an "incurable brain tumor", has been completely cured, with innovative `Immune` therapy.

Until recently, it was believed, that when Brain cells are lost in disorders such as Alzheimer's disease, that they were lost forever and not replaceable. But, happily, it has now been shown that new brain cells do form; it is because of this encouraging possibility, that I have been trying to `**stimulate her brain to think**` (aphorism -- use it, or lose it), by daily repeating the alphabet with her, telling her stories, and singing to her. *I honestly believe that we have markedly delayed the progression of her disease.* It is of note that we had previously tried all the available "Alzheimer medicines" early on, and found them to be ineffective, costly, and possibly dangerous.

Lastly, I believe that although `the Alzheimer patient` may appear unable to understand, or be able to comprehend the world around them, but I am reasonably sure, that they DO understand bits and pieces, even though their disease is far- advanced. It is now 9 years of her affliction, and although she is unable to talk coherently (only unintelligent babbles); she is much more alert, pleasant, and cooperative than she was four years ago.

Hopefully, I can `keep her going` until a cure is found.

Why not! They found a cure for brain tumors,
didn't they --- so, why not?

Is this wishful thinking?

Perhaps -- perhaps!

WHY, AND WHEN, TO WRITE A BOOK

Have you ever wondered why there are so many books in the world? Have you ever wondered where the material (words) that fills those million upon millions of pages that emerge as books, emanate? Well, the answer is really quite simple; those million upon millions of words are the wishes, loves, hates, questions, desires, etc. of people, like you and me.

The next question should be asked, why do so many millions of people feel compelled to "write stuff," anyway? Obviously, there must be hundreds, no thousands of reasons why a person or persons would feel compelled to bare their souls, for the entire world to see. Although the most frequent reasons are obvious i.e. for recognition, financial gain, and/or documentation, and dissemination of knowledge; but the writers I'm talking about are the non-professionals, who simply want to express themselves in the printed word. Not too long ago, I read about a young Japanese author who wrote two or three books a week. This unusual author, writing that many books in such a short period of time, required skill and talent, of course, but he surely had to utilize his writing schedule wisely. So, it appears, he wrote chapters for his current book while waiting for the bus, or waiting for his meal in a restaurant; and alas, even when the call of nature sounded. Perhaps the strangest and most spectacular aspect of this prolific writer's story is the fact that all of his stories are about `THE WILD WEST`, a land he had never visited, or seen! Oh, one more fact about this young writer – he always submitted his stories to be printed without ever proof reading them at least once. Now that's confidence!

At the outset of this discussion, I mentioned the fact that there are multitudes of reasons why a person or persons might want to express their feelings, or opinions, etc. into print (newspaper, journal, correspondence, and yes, books), so I will limit these futile ramblings to a few personal observations.

Several years ago, while I was still active in the practice of medicine, I, and all other medical physicians were required to keep abreast of advancing new medical knowledge, and were required to take written examinations

(Medical Boards) to demonstrate that we were qualified in our area of medical expertise. To say that the examinations were difficult would be a gross understatement, but we all agreed that the tests were fair – certainly necessary – and devilishly clever! It wasn't too unusual for many of the test-taking aspirants to fail the test at least once, because, as I previously stated, the tests were devilishly clever in their presentation; but most of the test takers did pass the examination after one or more attempts. However, there was one hardy soul who did try to pass the examination thirteen times, only to fail the test thirteen times. The strange part of this unfortunate saga was that this particular physician was one of the best Doc's around; he simply couldn't take a test. But, perseverance paid off, he did pass the examination on the fourteenth attempt. But, hold on, there is more to this heroic doctor's story; he subsequently wrote, and had published, an informative book -- with the title – yes -- "HOW TO PASS A MEDICAL EXAMINATION"! I really have no idea if his book was a best-seller or not, but I do know that this perseverant, astute physician continued to do good works that we / all physicians who knew him, would be proud to emulate.

As mentioned earlier, there are many reasons why an individual would want, or need, to submit his or her most intimate thoughts to print; I will now, for better or worse, tell you why, and when, I decided to submit to print my short stories; stories that literally encompass all aspects of my 87 years of life on this planet. The immediate question of me would be, "why would ANYONE choose to expose their most intimate thoughts, and life story, for the world to see? The answer to that difficult question can only be answered with one word – and that word is -- BECAUSE! Let me explain.

During my early years I, as most aspiring young people do, spent all of my energies just trying to decide who I was, and to survive the best way I could. Serendipity permitted me to seek an education that eventually resulted in a Medical degree from the Ohio State School of Medicine. I spent many years preparing myself to be a capable Medical Doctor; the following years of medical practice, and raising a family were rewarding and happy years. Then, without warning, my young daughter was struck a fatal blow (pulmonary embolus), and my world collapsed. It was while in deep emotional despair that I wrote a true story about two white ducks, and their valiant friend, a very large Canada goose. It was after I had witnessed the sudden death of one of the two white ducks, that I dedicated my story "IN MEMORY OF A DUCK" to my own, lost little duck.

After writing that first story, I began writing short stories to save my sanity. My subsequent stories were of everyday encounters with people, animals and nature; I never thought, or ever planned, to have them published. I had written the stories FOR ME; moreover, I really didn't think the stories that I had written were good enough quality to be published.

Several years after the terrible loss of my loved one, I experienced another devastating loss that changed my life forever; my wife had slowly descended into the 'world of shadows', she was afflicted with a mind and body stealing malady known as Alzheimer's disease. It was the ensuing battle with this merciless enemy that impelled me to write stories such as: "DESCENDING INTO THE WORLD OF SHADOWS", "WHERE HAVE THEY ALL GONE", and "MANY GOOD-BYES"; and, yes, our life, and Love Story, "AN ENDURING LOVE AFFAIR" -- to celebrate our sixty-two years of happy marriage.

So, yes, I had much earlier determined why I needed to write stories, now I had an epiphany why I needed to publish my stories. I realized that the malady (Alzheimer's disease had become an epidemic scourge in our society, and needed to be fought, and conquered. It somehow didn't matter that my stories would never win a Pulitzer Prize in Literature, or make a lot of money; if just one person benefited emotionally, or if my stories could in some small way help to continue mankind's awareness of this fearsome adversary, my efforts will not have been in vain.

PS,
    My three books are published under the Trilogy title:

LODFOC'S STORIES SHORT AND SWEET:
With subtitles:
Book I – Medical and personal views
Book II – Fish Tales and stories of the unusual
Book III – An Octogenarian's Oracles

SO, WHY CAN'T WE DREAM?

How does one begin a story about a subject that is so elusive and ethereal, as DREAMS? No, I am not talking about dreams that may, or may not, have substance; I am referring to dreams of the many, many years of happiness we have enjoyed together in wedded bliss; so, why can't we dream? It is the "miracle" of the human mind that enables us to preserve and recall the "what was" a life-time of happiness; even though destiny has now interfered, and torn our lives asunder. My dear wife has been afflicted with a malady (Alzheimer's disease) that has destroyed her brain and stolen her memory; she no longer lives in the reality of today; she exists, sadly, in a "world of shadows" where there are no yesterdays, or tomorrows.

Remarkably, a serendipitous event occurred at the nursing home one afternoon that presented an opportunity for me to penetrate my wife's world of tears; one of the staff's young members brought her beautiful infant son, Jace, to the nursing home for a brief time. The look on my wife's face, when she saw the child, was a look that I hadn't seen, for such a long time. She was smiling from ear to ear; it was a smile that was reminiscent of the smile that I had observed many years ago. It was a smile that I happily remember, when, after delivering our son, I held him up for her to see, and proclaimed, "Look honey, we have a beautiful baby boy!" Perhaps, for just a moment, the shroud of shadows that have enveloped her mind had parted, for her to briefly see and appreciate the reality of yesteryear.

For the past many months, my wife and I have shared many dreams of our past life together; I have read to her about places and things, that in the past, were valued and very important to us; although I'm not sure how many of those dreams were meaningful, or understood by her. Yet, she seemed to be pleased to hear stories recounting our life's experiences, and honestly, seems to be a happier person when hearing stories of past events.

It is true that her illness is gradually injuring and destroying her brain cells and cerebral electrical pathways; but, it is also true that new brain cells, and new brain cell interconnections can possibly develop when properly stimulated. The aphorism "Use it, or lose it" has never been truer.

Tragically, it is true that my wife and I will never again experience, or be able to create new memorable dreams in our life time, but re-counting, and enjoying our past happiness's will sublimate, and better, a terrible void in my life, and hopefully, make her life happier, and possibly, prolong her life. So -----

WHY CAN'T WE DREAM?

WINNERS AND LOSERS OF THE WORLD

It really should not come as a surprise to learn that we, all inhabitants of this world -- are, one way or another, winners AND losers. Who, of us, could say that they had never been disappointed or frustrated when they didn't succeed at an endeavor, or didn't receive the trophy after a contest; or, had been ecstatic, that their efforts had finally won first place awards in the competition? Yes, we, all citizens of the world, have won, and lost; or, will, have won or lost something, sometime, during our life's journey -- after all, we are only human, not so?

Well, if it a fact that we all are winners or losers at some place and time during our lives -- why discuss it -- why not let it go -- case closed. Ah, but not so fast, there is so much more to winning or losing, than winning and losing; would it not be HOW we accepted the win or lose that determines the true consequences, and importance, of the win or loss.

*Consider therefore: There are **winners** that are **true winners**; there are **winners** that are **true losers**; there are **losers** that are **true winners**, and unfortunately, there are **losers** that are **true losers**. But, how can that be? Isn't a loser -- a loser, and a winner a winner? The answer is yes, and no -- it all depends.*

To be sure, we all will win sometimes, and we all, will lose sometimes, but, as previously mentioned, it isn't the win or loss that determines whether one is a winner or loser, rather, it is how we personally, psychologically managed that win or loss that matters -- and determines who of us are the TRUE winners, and who of us are, alas, the TRUE losers. The following real-life-situations will hopefully clarify, and help us understand these seemingly dichotomous (contradictory) statements -- let's let a game of golf be our guide...

The winner of the PGA four day golf tournament was presented with the winner's cup and a check for $oooooo$. He, with a happy smile, said, "I am happy that I won, but I know that on another day, many of you would easily have beaten me." Yes, this man is a winner -- a TRUE

WINNER in the tournament of life; OR, alas, if, when he was presented with the winner's cup, said, "Well, it's about time I won, I knew there wouldn't be anyone here that could beat me". Yes, this man is a winner (of a golf tournament) -- but is sadly, a TRUE LOSER in the tournament of life!

But, in every contest, and in many of life's endeavors, there are losers (not winning in a contest); so what can be said about that a person who loses the contest (the player who was the `runner-up` in the contest)? Ah, the answer is determined by asking the losing player to say a few words. If the loser of the contest comments: "I am sorry to have not played well enough to win today, but I am happy for my competitor who played so well, and deserved to win. Yes, this man is a LOSER (lost the game), but is a TRUE WINNER in the tournament of life. Lastly, if the loser of the competition had said: "It was a lousy golf course to play on, and I should have won; I WILL win the next time". This loser of the competition is a TRUE LOSER in the tournament of life.

So, what is one to make of the confusing behavior of the various participants? How could there be such a variance of attitude and behavior? I don't know, maybe for some folks, the stars in the heavens had lost their brightness; or, perhaps, their DNA was misdirected. But, for the misfit who won the game, but lost the tournament of life (I am THE GREATEST AND THE BEST), the answer may not rest with the brightness of the stars, but, it might lie squarely with their upbringing. Consider: If a narcissistic parent (self-loving, conceited, self-important), raised a narcissistic off-spring, would you not have ` a possible winner of a game, or enterprise --- and have a loser in the tournament of life`?

Ah, yes, --- does it not appear, that being a winner
or a loser in the poker game of life ---

May well be,

A game of chance?

YOU ARE MY SUNSHINE

There are songs that make us happy, and there are songs that make us sad; and, I guess it is true, that buried in their lyrics or embryos, have a story to tell. It is universally agreed, that music can penetrate deeply into our subconscious souls, and may often change our overt conscious behavior. Yes, and so too, is it true with my song `You are my sunshine`; it truly does have a wonderful story to tell.

Yes, there are many songs in our lives that are listened to, but are not heard (goes in one ear, and out the other), but then at some later time, under different circumstances, that same tune is listened to carefully -- and blessedly, is gratefully heard. And, such, was the case for me and my renditions of the song "YOU ARE MY SUNSHINE".

Although, I think everyone in the world has probably heard the song `You are my sunshine` (either with this title, or a similar one), but nevertheless, I will include the lyrics just in case there is a poor soul who hasn't been privileged to have heard it.

You are my sunshine, my only sunshine,

You make me happy, when skies are gray.

You'll never know dear, how much I love you,

Please -- don't take my sunshine away.

The other night dear, I dreamed I held you in my arms;

You'll never know dear, how much I love you.

Please -- don't take, my sunshine --- away.

A love song you say? Yes, but it is so much more. It can be a soothing balm for a tortured brain, when under attack by a merciless enemy known as Alzheimer disease, or some other devastating infirmity.

Several years ago, my wife of many years (64), was afflicted with a malady known as Alzheimer's disease. Early on, she initially experienced minimal mental aberrations such as mild confusion, and forgetfulness, but as the months and years pasted, she became much more confused, erratic in behavior, and combative. It is well known medically, that combative behavior is common in Alzheimer's disease, and that successful treatment of the disease and combative behavior, is oft` times difficult without sedative medications. Ah, but what if there was a song that could soothe the uncontrolled inferno that is raging within the helpless breast? Yes, the song, `You are my sunshine`, works its miracle.

Now, my `sunshine miracle`

There have been many antidotal stories attributed to music as being a "cure" medicine that is able to soothe, or counteract, the deleterious effects of many medical maladies; how wonderful would it be, if I could help her combat her malignant `internal demon` with -- MY love, and *sound of music*.

For these past many years of our marriage, we would always laugh about the fact that my voice seemed to tranquilize her when I sang, or when I would read stories to her. Honestly, when reading to her and would look up, sure as shootin -- she would be sound asleep. So, I asked myself, would/could my singing subdue her Alzheimer's combative behavior; that self-question, was truly an epiphany, heaven sent; and, soon thereafter, made my life livable, and made possible, to be endured.

Let me assure you that my renditions of "You are my sunshine" are not praiseworthy; but, *they are* emotional and gently presented; and happily, **they do** put her `internal demons` to sleep. My musical renditions are rendered softly and quietly to her on a daily basis, prior to her luncheon time.

When I first gently sang my 'You are my shine' song to her, she acted as if I was bothering her, and appear uncomfortable, and look aimlessly around the room. I didn't know if it was my voice, or if it was the song that was the offending culprit; but never-the-less, I continued to sing to her. As the days and months pasted, my daily renditions continued. It was gratifying to see, even after the first few days of my luncheon serenades, that she seemed to *want* to hear me sing, OUR song, and *wanted,* to look at me as I sang to her. Remarkably, she has gradually, become less combative; and now, when I sing to her, she will even reach out to me, as I render MY loving, 'sunshine song' to *her.*

Today, yes, today, I continue to sing to her at luncheon time, and we will often acknowledge each other -- *by rubbing noses* as I sing to her (it is an endearing custom of greeting & affection) that we observed many years ago when we had visited the Maori Indians, of New Zealand).

And, so, it would appear, that the miracle of --- Love and music --

Are powerful antidotes -- for the many 'toxins' of life!

YOU NEVER KNOW

If one were to ask "What do you think will happen in the future", I'm sure you would look questioningly, and then look your questioner straight in the eye, and exclaim "What? Are you nuts"? If I had been asked that same question, I would have shouted out "If I knew what will be in the future -- I'D BE KING!" Of course, my latter remarks are an emphatic figure of speech, but I would let him know how foolish the question is, since those three words are the `stuff of dreams`, and merits no response.

Ah, but we would be wise to more carefully analyze the meaning of the underlying question, since the answer is, truly, -- YOU NEVER KNOW! Perhaps the answer should be -- "**what will be, will be**".

Since it would seem that we will never know `what will be` in the future; does that mean we are hostages awaiting judgment? No, of course not, but, it does mean that the wise individual should carefully, and quickly measure each circumstance occurring in life, and watch for the possibility of future `happenings`. Would it not be sensible to think that "what I do now, could possibly influence future `happenings`? For sure! What I have been trying to say, in a round- about way, is, "think before you act, and don't do something stupid!"

Oh, sure, there will be many `you never knows` that are encountered during our lives, that will confound our inner souls; but really, shouldn't we be just a little indignant, and exclaim, with an empathic "we shall see about that"; then -- then open all valves and do what destiny will allow us to do?

It is an amazing thing that often happens when we are confronted by the words, "you never know"; especially, when we need to be certain of our future direction in life, and thus will be able to fulfill our destinies.

It seems, at times, that our future paths in life are `carved in stone`, and our direction in life, is unalterably pre-determined; such was the case of a young man who was born during the depression years of the 1920 -1930's, and who had suffered the relentless torment of the severe depression of those terrible years and then, alas, followed by the horrific devastation of World War II, of the 1940's.

Although the depression, and the following war years were fearful, they did galvanize the survival instincts of the citizenry; and so, our young man, prematurely ---"grew-up", and realized that having an education was essential if there ever was a hope of being a Medical Doctor (he had been a medical corpsman during the war, and had resolved to become a doctor).

It was at this juncture of his life, that he was to make the most meaningful decision of his life; he enrolled in a local College's Premed program.

It was during his first visit with the school appointed Premed Advisor that he heard the words `one never knows`. It was at that meeting, that he made a decision that would determine his future direction in life. Yes, it was during that first meeting, that his advisor, after reading our young man's previous high school scholarship records, looked up at him and asked, "Son, why do you want to go to college?" The question startled the young man, but he answered softly "Sir, I want to be a doctor". The advisor then sighed, looked down at the high school records he was holding, and said, "Son, why don't you learn to do something with your hands", and then continued to say, "Although **one never knows**, I think you would be wasting your time". Our young man was devastated when he heard those words, but he did realize that his early school grades were abysmal. He then answered in a barely perceptible voice, "Sir, the records you are holding were compiled when times were stressful, and the person who had compiled those awful scholarship records, is gone forever". He, then in tears, looked at the advisor, and confidently said, "Well, Sir, it would be my time that I'd be wasting -- why can't I try; the advisor, remained quiet for the longest time, and then said, **"Sure. Why not, we won't know -- until you try."**

And, yes, he did try. He tried honestly, and intensively; he never, ever considered the possibility of failure.

The following twelve years were a witness to the transformation of a determined young man who gradually matured into a person who gratefully accepted the responsibilities of being a Medical Physician. Those twelve years, were difficult twelve years; but saw him earn a Bachelor Degree at Ohio University; a Medical Degree at Ohio State University; a one year Internship, and then, followed by a three year Internal Medicine Residency at Akron General Medical Center.

Finally, finally, he was able to answer the question that had plagued him for so long, "WOULD HE EVER KNOW if he would/ could be a Medical Physician? He slowly answered, with a wry smile on his face --

"You never know; why can't I try?"

PS,

Yes, our young man, Andrew Opritza, Md, FACP (Lofdoc) practiced Internal Medicine, honorably, for over thirty years. Now, in the twilight years of his life (age, 89), he was asked, "What would your thoughts be when you hear the three words; ` **You never know**`? His answer --

WE'LL SEE ABOUT THAT!

PS,

The cryptic meaning of the words `YOU NEVER KNOW` is so terribly important in everyday life, and commerce. Consider: An elderly, shabbily attired gentleman enters an automobile dealership, and proceeds to look at various cars on display. Although he had been looking for a considerable time, the majority of the dealership salesman made it plain by their actions that they thought `the old man` was just a poor old man who was only looking, and not worth wasting their time with him.

Interestingly, as the old man was about to leave the car showroom, a young man, just returning from his lunch break, ran over to the departing, frustrate old gentleman and asked him "Sir, Did you find what you were looking for, could I help you?

Yes, you guessed right. The old man was a multi-millionaire, and bought a fleet of 50 cars for his mega corporation -- from the young man.

Honest,

YOU NEVER KNOW!

Why don't you try?

Printed in the United States
By Bookmasters